Confessions
of a
Non-Charismatic

SEEKING A SPIRIT-FILLED LIFE

Confessions of a
Non-Charismatic

SEEKING A SPIRIT-FILLED LIFE

KEN ANDERSON

innovative
Christian Publications

Grand Haven, Michigan

Published by Innovative Christian Publications Division
Baker Trittin Press
P. O. Box 20
Grand Haven, Michigan 49417

The Holy Bible, KING JAMES VERSION

HOLY BIBLE, NEW INTERNATIONAL VERSION, copyright
1973, 1978, 1984 by International Bible Society

Confessions of a Non-Charismatic
By Ken Anderson

To order additional copies please call 616-846-8550
or email info@btconcepts.com
http://www.gospelstoryteller.com

Publishers Cataloging- Publication Data
Anderson, Ken, 1917-
        Confessions of a Non-Charismatic /
        Ken Anderson - Grand Haven, Michigan: Baker Trittin
Press
                p. cm.
Library of Congress Control Number: 2003116936
        ISBN: 0-9729256-7-8
        1. Autobiography 2. Religious 3. Holy Spirit
        I. Title II. Confessions of a Non-Charismatic
BIO018000

Printed in the United States of America
Cover: Paul S. Trittin

To
Mrs. A
whose
footsteps
follow
the
footprints
of angels

Table
of
Contents

FOREWORD

In this day of puff personal stories, whether biographies, autobiographies or media sound bites, you'll find this book refreshing. Ken Anderson's confessions have mercifully sidestepped both self-flagellation and self-aggrandizement.

I consider Ken Anderson one of the most transparent Christian leaders I have met in the course of my 80 years. In my view, he could not bring himself to put his brilliant insights or prodigious activities in a light slanted to enhance either.

Years ago, I heard a history professor, at the time president of a famous university, say that historians agreed there were only three honest autobiographies: Augustine, Rousseau and Trotsky. To those three, I would have to add John Wesley — and now, Ken Anderson.

What a marvelous insight Ken gives the reader in delineating the harsh experience of his childhood and adolescence. The first chapter, "Father and Son," makes the measure of the man.

Chapter 12 reveals his experience in Stockholm. I believe many charismatic friends, when reading this, will say to themselves, "Ken is a charismatic even though he doesn't know it!"

For more than a quarter of a century, Ken Anderson lectured in Singapore and in Maui to credentialed world leaders from more than 150 countries. The credentialed leaders to whom he has lectured include media moguls, urban planners, vice presidents of nations, parliamentarians, Supreme Court judges, business tycoons, university presidents — in short, men and women who have a large part in determining the course of their respective nations.

Whether they were Catholics, Calvinists or Charismatics, they immediately felt drawn to him. Hundreds of these world leaders still maintain contact with him.

Ken's many years in dealing with Christian believers of every intellectual rank, every social stratum and every cultural echelon, uniquely qualifies him to write this book. He has plumbed experiences and forged insights every thoughtful, investigative Christian believer needs to know.

Though living modestly and out of the limelight in his delightful Indiana town, Ken is known and sought by people around the world. I can't name a dozen American writers who are known by as many people — in an intimate, face-to-face relationship — as Ken Anderson.

Read this book carefully. Then reread it. Make notations in the margins. Underline the passages that speak to you. Then adapt the lessons learned to enhance your relationships with all believers. Surely that will go a long way in fulfilling the high priestly prayer of our Lord in John 17, "That they may be one."

I plan to give this book several readings.

Dr. John Edmund Haggai
Haggai Institute
December, 2003

FOREWARN

The good life in our Lord Jesus Christ! That's what it's all about. If charismatic manifestations come naturally for you as a Christian, so be it. Why change?

However, if you desire fulfillment beyond anything you have ever known, why wait for a specific manifestation to occur before you claim God's fullness as part of your natural life style?

You will invariably find a considerable difference between a non-charismatic Christian and an *anti*-charismatic one. Maturing Christians realize that the Apostle Paul, the primary writer of charismatic teaching in the Bible, obviously speaks of the inspiration of the Holy Spirit as in 1 Corinthians 13:12, he writes, . . .*now we see through a glass darkly; but then face-to-face; now I know in part, but then shall I know even as also I am known.* Isn't it unique for Paul to have been given these very words in the heart of the epistle to the Corinthians in which he expounds charismatic theology?

There are many believers from the charismatic movement with whom I enjoy fellowship. During my extended lifetime, I have served on local and national boards involving believers of both persuasions who ministered together with mutually enriching camaraderie.

My purpose in writing this book is to illustrate a significant truth, namely this:

1. Simply by following the plain teaching of the Bible, children of God (any individual or ministering group) may personally experience the fullness of the Holy Spirit in their lives without the prerequisite of charismatic manifestations.

2. You will find by reading further that in no way do I so much as imply that one should avoid charismatic manifestations. Settle for nothing less than God's best for you . . . whatever that may be!

These Scriptures have been especially helpful to me as I was seeking the Spirit-filled life.

Whether you eat or drink or whatever you do, do it all to the glory of God.   1 Corinthians 10:31

The fruit of the Spirit is love, joy, peace, patience, kindness, goodness, faithfulness, gentleness, self-control.   Galatians 5:22-23

Trust in the Lord with all your heart, and do not lean on your own understanding. In all your ways acknowledge Him, and He will make your paths straight.   Proverbs 3:5-6

One of the manifestations commonly associated with charismatics is divine healing. But that is not foreign to most Christian denominations. In that arena, I have some amazing events to share subsequently with you in chapter ten, but now I want to reveal a very personal experience concerning healing.

For months I had been enduring severe pain in my legs and feet, and we were visiting doctors trying to find the cause. During that extended time period, I had surgery and my gallbladder was removed. While I was in the hospital, the doctor in charge spoke to Mrs. A. "Do you think there is any possibility Mr. Anderson has Parkinson's?" She voiced her agreement.

In 1997 it was a definite diagnosis. I had Parkinson's. Two years earlier I was diagnosed with diabetes, and it was controlled by medication. But Parky, as I call it, is a malady that seemed to wait for a formal declaration before it launched its nasty talents.

I did not pray for healing, only God's will.

I remember one time there was a famous healing evangelist on television, and he was telling people to just trust the Lord for healing. As he talked, I asked the Lord to heal me. I had some peace that maybe it really happened, but it didn't.

Another day I awakened in the early morning hours having dreamed I was healed. In my dream I walked up and down the stairs two or three steps at a time. In my awakened state I checked my legs and seemed to have my balance. Mrs. A awakened and I announced, "I'm healed." For a few days I had this freedom, and then the characteristics of Parky returned.

I concluded God had selected an illness for my denouement.

I am blessed . . . yes, I mean genuinely blessed . . . by what I call my denouement illness, that is, the Great Physician has been pleased to afflict my body with conditions that will inevitably terminate my life. But it is a long process. I still have many books I want to write, and I know I will have the time to do all the writing God has for me. I am buoyed by the promise Christ has given.

I will not leave you comfortless.
I will come to you. John 14:18

Let us move on to experience and learn how to make the Bible valid and functional for each of us. If you have questions or experiences of your own to share, I would be pleased to keep in touch.

Ken Anderson, February. 2004

ONE

Father Versus Son

I once groveled in self-sympathy, bestowing upon myself a mile wide, canyon deep persecution complex. Fomenting this were earliest childhood memories of obese ladies from our church patting me on the head and lamenting, "Poor li'l Kennut, your mama died. But Yesus take care of li'l Kennut, yah."

I especially remember Yarda Strandberg, fattest of them all, who would draw me face first against her blubbery torso until I struggled to free myself lest I suffocate.

But I need to explore wider areas of my childhood to understand my early spiritual moorings as they relate to the gratifying Christian life I live today.

I make no claim of being an abused child. My father was a strict disciplinarian. He kept a switch above the wall clock in our living room and used it painfully and strenuously. *"Foolishness is bound up in the heart of a child,"* he quoted (Proverbs 22:15), *"but the rod of correction will drive it far from him.* He was many times more cruel to animals, his instrument of discipline being a triple-tined pitchfork which he jammed into the undersides of a horse or cow that displeased him. As for what I may have suffered by way of emotional wounds, I have long ago dismissed from my considerations.

I do insist my father played a strategic role in the shaping of my religious background in general and subsequently became cause and effect in regard to attitudes I developed concerning charismatic influences. How they may have shaped my adult thinking I leave to the evaluation of others.

I need to establish the fact that my father and I had bad vibes from our very first day together. Here's a hasty sum of what happened.

I was born on a farm in northwest Iowa at sunup of a blustery late December day. By afternoon, my mother was stricken with what was later presumed to be uremic poisoning. The ten rural miles to the nearest doctor lay in the vice-like grip of snow that had been drifting persistently throughout the day. Stella, my mother's sister, maintained liaison with our family doctor until strong winds broke the main service line from town, silencing rural phones.

My mother had been in excruciating pain for several hours. By late afternoon, she lapsed into a coma. But as the sun set, she opened her eyes, gasped, then settled back onto her pillow. Silence permeated the front room in which a bed had been set up to make the delivery of the baby and the subsequent caring for my mother as convenient as possible.

After several moments of silence, my grandmother began to wrestle the blankets covering her daughter.

"Oh!" she gasped as she searched for her daughter's pulse. "I think maybe . . . ."

Tense silence overtook the farmhouse interior . . . only for a moment.

"Goodbye, Ethel," Grandma whispered. Turning to my father, she added in tears, "Oh, Oscar! Our darling is gone! She's with Jesus!"

"No! no!" my father cried out. Impetuously, he threw himself onto the bed, awakening his newborn son.

"Go ahead, kid!" he bellowed. "Bawl! It's your fault, y'know!"

"Oscar!" Stella rebuked. "What kind of insanity is talk like that?"

Even as she corrected her brother-in-law, whom she despised, Stella moved to the bed and covered her sister's face with the sheet.

My mother's funeral was one of the biggest community events of the year, its magnitude expanded by reports that I also had died and would lie nested in my mother's arm. During the prior night, a full-scale blizzard had struck with unrelenting force, blocking the entire town and countryside. At normal times this would have meant postponement of the funeral. In our case, it was different. The drama of the event gripped attention of the entire community. As a result, at early dawn tractors were seen towing discs, harrows, and sundry makeshift elements. Together with a virtual army of men armed with scrapers, scoops, and shovels, they opened roads which otherwise would have remained unchallenged.

An hour and a half prior to the announced time of the funeral, streams of people . . . most of them on foot . . . were moving toward the Swedish Free Church. The sanctuary had standing room only by the time the bell began tolling out the twenty-six years of my mother's short time on earth.

During the pre-service viewing, an outspoken local madame took one look into the casket, jabbed an angry elbow into her husband's ribs, and exclaimed, "Ain't that the limit, Ardmore? Ain't it now? We make all this effort t'get here only t'find it ain't no different from yer ordinary funerals. C'mon, we're goin' home before I lose my manners!"

As everyone expected, the funeral would best be described as a time of intense emotion. The moment the pastor stepped to the pulpit and said, "Oscar, Grandmother, and family, our hearts weep with you on this sad day," an enormous empathy claimed every individual present.

Funerals were a social event and each burial became a unique event in its own way.

"What shall we do with the baby?" my father asked his mother-in-law after the interment. "We could put him in that new orphanage our church helps sponsor over in Nebraska."

"It's time for me to tell you something," Grandma began. (Actually, even among people not members of the Anderson clan, she was affectionately known as "Granny.")

Granny hesitated, gathered her thoughts, then continued, "Last summer Ethel came to me. She was sure she was bearing a son. She asked me to promise I would take care of him if something ever happened to her."

"At your age?" my dad scoffed lightly. "Let's just send him to the orphanage and be shed of it."

"I promised my daughter!" Granny insisted. "It's a sacred trust!"

I moved in with Granny at her house in town, seldom seeing my father.

Granny was kind and patient. On the occasional Sundays when my dad attended church, she always invited him to stop at our home for dinner. At first he refused, then he occasionally agreed. Eventually it became a regular event. During none of those early visits did he ever show any interest in me. One Sunday Granny boldly suggested that she and I come to the farm, and she could fix some weekday meals there. He reluctantly acquiesced.

I fell in love with the farm. When we went to help him, my curiosity got the better of me, and I began following him around his chore route among the buildings. Happening enough times for it to become a childhood memory, he would reach down and take my hand. More often he ignored me completely.

It became obvious my dad lacked skills for handling both farming and household responsibilities. Granny became the farm's volunteer cleaning lady. She did the laundry. She scrubbed the floors. The time came when she and I would spend nearly a week of each month at the farm.

The inevitable happened. Following one lengthy session in the country, the time passed when we ordinarily returned to her house in town. My father mentioned it to her.

"You want us to go?" she asked.

"Well, uh . . ." my father searched for words.

Forthrightly, Granny said, "I'm sure the best way for me to fulfill my pledge to Ethel is for her darling boy and me to close up the house in town and come to the farm to work alongside you."

The first phase seemed a total success.

"You've sure done a good job with the kid so far," my dad complimented. "He follows me around, watches what I do."

"That's the way we want it to be," Granny said, choking lightly.

By the time I began school, I was handling many of the barnyard chores . . . spreading ensilage for the cattle, pitching hay to the horses, tossing corn ears to the hogs.

Doing chores put me at right angles with my dad. He activated the old syndrome of his attitude toward me. One day, for example, I was running a bit late on my work. To hasten completion of my chores so that I could finish in time to go into the house for the "Lum and Abner" radio show, I skimped on the corn that I threw to the hogs not realizing my dad was watching from a secluded spot nearby.

"Can't you do nothin' right?" he yelled at me.

His words cut like a machete. It became a syndrome, the explosive tirades from my father, not to mention frequent trips to the whipping switch atop the dining room clock.

By the time I reached the age of ten, vacation months from school involved hard work in the fields. During mid-summer, oppressive heat often made field activity during daylight hours virtually impossible. At 3 a.m. during haying season, for example, my dad would get me up. We hitched a team of horses to the hay rack, hung lanterns on the rack for illumination as we gathered pile after pile of cured hay. He pitched the hay up to me and I smoothed it out onto the rack. As we took each load back to the barn, I would fall dead asleep on the hay, awakening at barn side to help transfer the fragrant alfalfa into the loft.

Granny was my sustaining angel. She had had less than two years of school, yet she read Shakespeare to me. She loved history. We had a couple of PBS radio stations nearby, and through her, I became a fan of classical music. The two of us rarely missed Wayne King every Thursday night. In the quiet evenings and during inclement weather, she helped me enjoy the wonders of nature.

For example, when we reached our observation post and watched the dusk descend outside, she would urge me not to miss the changing tones of grass and trees. We had a running contest to determine who would see the first star of evening. A thunderstorm at night turned both of us into uncompromised aesthetics as lightening bolts tore open the sky like rending sword thrusts. Falling rain doubled the majesty of the spectacle. To this day, when other people complain about stormy weather, I stand at a rain-splattered window and look out at the breathtaking drama of a so-called nasty night.

"Well, how is Granny's little farmer?" she would ask when I came home bone weary from a hard day in the fields.

On the contrary, I could not recall a time when my father complimented me for anything I did.

By the time I reached high school, I became proficient in sports. I was named to the All County Basketball Team and also set the school record for running the mile in a hearty four minutes forty-five seconds. My dad became an avid fan, and I was slightly bewildered when one day, after we had won a hard game, I actually overheard him bragging about his son.

At home, it was a different matter. "You ain't worth your salt," became increasingly familiar. When I was a junior in high school, the two of us got into a violent quarrel. I picked up a bucket of ice-cold water and dumped it over him. Insanely angry, he lunged at me. But I caught him in a head lock and wrestled him to the ground. I can yet remember the look on his face as he tried to lift up and wrest himself free from my complete subjugation of him.

"Please, Kenny," he whispered, "I'm getting an awful headache."

I remember a hiatus after that skirmish. The chain of command had definitely changed at the farm. He became downright obsequious at times.

I remember how deftly Granny took me aside.

"Please be nice to your dad."

Because of the profound respect I had for this woman, her voice took on distinct authority. "You will soon be graduating from high school," she added. "You will be leaving home and heading for college. You . . ."

"College?" I interrupted. "I put college out of my mind over a year ago."

It was the first time I had ever stood up to my grandmother. I wanted to apologize, but I had much too much pride for that.

"I'll see what I can do," I said, sulking away.

Granny looked at me for a long moment. Slowly a smile etched her lips as she said, "You will be going to college."

About this time, my dad and I had begun playing checker games at night. It was excellent release, and I didn't too much mind that he beat me resoundingly every game. Actually, my dad was kind of the local champion. Other men came to our house to challenge him. He never lost. I can hear him yet, giggling as he won contest after contest.

One day, someone heard about a checker shark in the Norwegian community next to ours. I should mention that our entire county was characterized by settlements whose identity and loyalty went back to European origins. There were also German communities, Finnish, and Danish.

This Norwegian gentleman had actually come to be thought of as the county champ.

An amazing thing happened. I actually found myself becoming one of my dad's fans. On the night of the championship match, held uptown at one of the tables in Crone Brothers' Confectionary, a sizable crowd gathered to see what would happen.

It would be the best two games out of three.

The Norwegian, Thorwald Gunnarsen, won the first match with no problem.

My dad was astounded. His cheeks turned crimson.

Although I had never beaten my father in a game played just between ourselves, I was giving him consistently better competition and had a sneaking hunch I would beat him one day.

On this night of Swedes versus Norwegians I had especially watched Thorwald Gunnarsen and had learned his simple strategy which I related to my dad.

"Good for you, boy!" He put his arm across my shoulder, showing me the first intimacy, scant though it was, in all our years together.

The next moment, Thorwald Gunnarsen called out, "Ve got vun more nudder games to play!"

"Two more," my dad corrected. Thorwald looked at my father a moment, "Yah," he laughed, "two games, I already vun the fust. Let's us git goin' now on number two!"

Silence fell across the crowd as the second game began. In the first moment of my dad's effort . . . following my instructions . . . he gave away one and got two for himself.

By that one show of expertise, the Norwegian was mortally wounded and . . . playing it cool . . . my dad won.

The two were tied one game each!

In the rubber match, my dad won even more handily!

That might have healed things between the two of us except that the following evening my dad wanted to play a game with me.

I beat him!

I beat him in the second game, too.

We never played again, and the rapport we had built with each other waned.

Granny saw what happened and tried to move in as peacemaker.

"It's no use, Granny," I muttered.

Our primary battlegrounds became the barn where we milked the cows, the feeding lot where we fattened the hogs, and the chicken coop and such. Usually we did the chores together, but sometimes he would sneak off at chore time and leave the responsibilities completely with me.

We had such a heated argument one time, I'm sure we would have come to blows. Granny, however, having had all she could bear of the seething hatred, burst into such bitter sobbing I felt sure she was going to have a heart attack.

I turned heel and sprinted away.

Usually I regained my calm after such tirades, but not this time. Far into the following night, I tossed in my bed unable to sleep.

It was about four o'clock when I rolled out of bed, got dressed, and stumbled outside. First, I jogged around a couple of our fields, and this helped. It didn't change my mental attitude, but I'm sure my blood pressure came down.

When I got back to the buildings, I sauntered into the tool shed. It was full morning by now, and I could see items in the shed. At about the same moment, two things happened.

The door opened, and my dad came out of the house calling

my name in an obviously bad mood.

At the same moment, I saw the single shot rifle I had bought for two bits at a farm sale.

Subconsciously, almost, I opened the rifle, selected a bullet and loaded the gun.

Again my dad called my name.

"Kenny, you hear me! Get yourself up here! We got work to do. There's fence that needs fixin'. Get your tools all together so you can take care of it right away after breakfast."

Just then, he took a few steps toward the barn, bringing him into perfect range outside the tool shed door.

I cocked the rifle, lifted it to my shoulder, and took aim.

It would be so easy . . . so very easy.

I took perfect aim at his head, slipped my finger onto the trigger and then . . . in my mind, I heard a woman's voice. I don't remember a thing she said, but . . . it remains strong in my memory . . . the softness, the persuasive beauty . . . could it have been my mother calling to me from Heaven?

My dad stood motionless. All I had to do was tighten my finger on the trigger.

I can't explain why. But I couldn't do it.

Slowly, I put down the gun and walked out of the tool shed directly into my father's presence.

He lashed out at me like a striking snake, reminding me of the fence needing repair.

"Get your stuff together like I told you!" he stormed.

I turned around and walked into the tool shed hesitating a moment to look at the rifle.

Suddenly, reality hit me! My dad was gone, but as I looked out of the shed I saw where he had stood and realized how easy it would have been for him to be lying there . . . dead!

The nearest thing I had ever experienced to thanking God slipped silently from my lips. From that moment onward, I was finished with any more bad scenes involving my father.

Nevertheless, anger seethed inside me, anger that lasted through my years in college and on into my adult life.

Dreams often make lasting impressions. It was during my high school years, when I had no assurance of a relationship with God, that I had a very vivid dream. In my dream I was sitting outside our consolidated rural high school building with a friend as we were eating our lunches. An attractive girl my same age paused in front of me. When I looked up into her eyes she said, "When you get your life straightened out, you will find me." Then she was gone. My dream ended, but the memory lingered.

College?

Granny was determined that I attend Wheaton College in Illinois. She would provide the funds.

"Don't talk to the kid about college," my dad implored his mother-in-law. "Let's keep him on the farm, then we'll all have security for the future."

Quietly, Granny sold her house in town and thus assured my education.

I arrived on the Wheaton College campus, a gawking, awkward country boy suddenly thrust into an environment alien to anything previously known or expected. However, as I walked across campus, thoughts of my high school dream returned solidly to my mind, and I began looking for the girl in my dream.

In the moments following my arrival at the house where I would stay, I met such students as Bob Evans and Carl Henry. Bob would one day establish Greater Europe Mission while Carl would join the ranks of the great contemporary theologians.

That first Sunday night, I rode into Chicago with a group of students to attend evening services at the famous Moody Memorial Church.

Dr. Harry Ironside, pastor of the church, preached a sermon on "assurance."

I was the first seeker to enter the Inquiry Room.

That night, Ken Anderson became assured of his relationship with the Man, Jesus Christ, who twenty centuries earlier had hung on a cross to make salvation the option for every human being!

I became an adult at Wheaton!

There was one shortcoming.

As year's end loomed, I received a letter from my grandmother. She wanted very much for me to continue at Wheaton, but her available funds could not bear the costs.

The possibility that I would be unable to continue at Wheaton College was another painful reminder of the girl in my high school dream. Now, I was about to leave college and I had not met her. My imminent departure brought the dream into focus and with it came a sense of depression.

During the summer months, through a series of circumstances I did not arrange, I was able to transfer to the Free Church School in Chicago, now known as Trinity University in Deerfield, Illinois.

As I approached the campus carrying my suitcase, I was suddenly startled by the girl in my dream. There she stood, Doris Jones, a sophmore from Nebraska. She paid me no attention, not even a glance, but I recognized her immediately as the girl of my dream.

Two additional years passed, and I returned to the Wheaton campus accompanied by the girl of my dream. She has been my wife for over 65 years!

I began writing with sufficient success to pay my way through Wheaton.

As a result of my writing, I was named managing editor of the

Youth for Christ Magazine, now known as Campus Life. The job offered such opportunities as ghost writing feature articles for a young evangelist named Billy Graham.

I was invited by Bob Pierce to accompany him on a trip to the Orient, to China, assisting in the production of a documentary motion picture which literally inspired the launching of World Vision.

China became a gigantic happening in my life.

When I left the United States, I was spiritually ill. Pride and vanity, like lethal cancers, were decimating my very soul.

Additionally, just before returning to Wheaton, Zondervan Publishing House had released my first novel, *Mystery of Parkview*. My head was swollen with pride.

LOOK OUT, WORLD! HERE COMES THE FUTURE AUTHOR OF THE GREAT CHRISTIAN NOVEL!

There was one problem. *Mystery of Parkview* was a total flop.

One reviewer wrote, "The writing is amateurish, the plot uninteresting, the characters ridiculous, and the mystery nonexistent."

My pride was sorely wounded, but I fought back.

My second novel, *The Doctor's Return*, though only slightly improved, sold thousands of copies over the next decade.

World War Two raged across Europe and gave me an idea for a love story centered in Norway. We named it *Shadows Under the Midnight Sun*.

This led to an opportunity to write scripts for a fledgling Christian film organization, which, in turn, resulted in the development of our own company.

Our film work involved the production of motion pictures which we rented to churches. We also did promotional films for Christian organizations. One of these was a prestigious assignment. The film, *Africa in Three Dimensions*, was produced for screening at an upcoming Mennonite World Congress in Amsterdam. Just as we finished filming in Kenya, I received a cable from my wife informing me that my dad was in the hospital, dying.

A Pan Am DC6 took painfully laborious hours covering the distance from Nairobi to New York. Those hours also involved my anguish over my long-lasting hatred of my father.

Doris met me at the airport in New York, and we drove all the way to the hospital in Iowa where my dad was mortally ill. To my amazement, he was stretched out on his bed reading the paper. I crossed the room. The television set blared loudly.

"What do you mean my dad is dying?" I demanded from the doctor the next day when he came for his morning rounds. We conferred in the hallway outside his room.

"Your father is an ox of a man," the doctor replied. "He has had at least a dozen heart attacks in the last two weeks, any one of which would have killed an ordinary person. He has deteriorated so rapidly, we're sure he'll die today."

His words startled me. I remember pacing up and down the hospital corridor, crying out to heaven. "God, my dad's dying. I have absolutely no love for him. Please don't let him die while I still hold this terrible hatred in my heart."

A miracle happened!

In those moments, I received an anointing. It was as though divine oil poured down from heaven coating the inside of my entire body.

It was warm.

It was captivating.

It was glorious!

As though escorted, I walked briskly back into my dad's room, entered, and stood at the foot of his bed for a silent moment. As he became aware of my presence, he put down his newspaper.

I tried to speak.

I couldn't.

A look of amazement came to my dad's countenance. His eyes widened as he stared at my face. I have no idea what he saw.

Lovingly, I reached for his feet and began massaging them. A look of sheer wonderment came to his eyes. He smiled with the loving expression of a father toward his son.

Then, suddenly, it happened. He began to choke. I rushed to the front of his bed.

It was my first encounter with death.

My dad had asked my wife, Doris, if he could come and live with us following his dismissal from the hospital. Faithfully and lovingly she had agreed.

Now abide faith, hope, and love: these three.
But the greatest of these is love.
1 Corinthians 13:13

That was over three decades ago. Yet, the love placed within my heart by the Holy Spirit that day has not so much as wavered once. I had a new appreciation and understanding of what this third person of the Trinity could do. The amazing outpouring of love that day placed within me a deep desire to seek all God had for me, a Spirit-filled life.

By this shall all men know you are my disciples,
if you love one another.
John 13:35

Two

The
Quiet
Way

I admit to feeling uncomfortable in a charismatic meeting. Is it because I am spiritually unfit? Or because I am by nature so overtly shy? There was a time in my fledgling experience when I found something of a sanctified envy in my heart toward the spiritual presence of charismatics. Their buoyant optimism and spiritual zest attested to their confidence in their Lord Jesus Christ.

You see, I am one of those laid back kind of guys who goes to a football game and sits in silence throughout the entire four quarters. My wife, meanwhile, reacts vocally with the playing out of a game. I tend to conduct myself similarly in public meetings, particularly those that occur in a sanctuary or an auditorium being used for a religious gathering.

This diffident nature has, through the years, touched every aspect of my communications with other people. I was shy of strangers. Shy of self-confident extroverts. Shy of leaders . . . people with exceptional talent . . . and terribly shy of girls . . . shy at times, almost to the point of disgust!

While I in no sense of the word accuse charismatics of being exhibitionists, any such conduct was on my personal taboo list. The point is, how could a shy Ken Anderson impose upon his inhibitions any public participation in what I thought were wild calisthenics often common to charismatic public worship.

As I became an adult, a new kind of annoyance settled in to fester my personality. That is, I could be shy and retiring in one set of circumstances, outgoing and hilarious in another. Splattered by goose-bumps at the sight of my own shadow, I could, in a subsequent moment, be a complete extrovert!

I tell you these things so you can more clearly understand and . . . I trust . . . empathize with me as I share my experiences in understanding the Holy Spirit. My primary goal has always been to attain a mature understanding and use of the Bible in learning to live a valid and satisfying Christian life.

During my earliest childhood years, I knew practically nothing about charismatics and their movement. As a matter of fact, we attended a Swedish Free Church in a small northwest Iowa town some five miles from our farm. Members considered themselves possessors of the absolute truth of the Bible . . . salvation by public response to an altar call, baptism by immersion, total separation from the world which included refraining from attendance at public theaters, dances, total abstinence from consumption of alcohol, smoking, card playing, and cursing. However, some of the holiest of Free Church folk were known for the uttering of blazing invectives in the Swedish language.

These mores drove an ever widening and deepening wedge of separation between the members of the Swedish Free Church and the Lutheran Church at the southern tip of the town. The Lutherans enjoyed freedom from the legalism required of Free Church members. Lutherans could go to movies. They could play cards. They could smoke. They could drink hard liquor.

You name it, Lutherans could do it!

As a matter of fact, the Free Church emphasized soul winning but not in sense of a man with his Bible walking the streets on a Sunday afternoon hoping to find someone with a heart hungry enough to be a candidate for transforming salvation. No, to the average Free Church member, witness was a synonym for abstinence.

There did seem to be some possible leniency to those who secretly kept a pinch of snuff . . . "snuce", it was called . . . below the lower lip. One of the most prominent members, proprietor of a successful dry goods and grocery store, was known for the partaking of "snuce" every day of the week except Sunday. It was also known that the leniency was due to the fact this gentleman gave his eight dollars every week to the support of the church, a substantial amount in those depression-ridden years.

Lutherans did not differentiate between non-Lutheran congregations. They did not dub congregations like our Free Church as fundamentalist, for example, such terminology not having reached as far West as northwest Iowa in those days.

Churches, the likes of ours, as well as any other separationist denomination were all swept into one designation.

But they were not called pentecostals.

We were all called *Holy Rollers*!

In my memory, however, in our county there were only four churches that we would label as Holy Roller today. Seven miles distance from our farm lay the village of Swea Center in which stood another of the Swedish Free Churches with which our church was affiliated. We occasionally visited this church of our denomination. Immediately across the street stood a small recently painted, yet ever so somewhat bedraggled, pentecostal edifice. On hot summer nights, especially when windows needed to be kept open, worshippers in our Swea Center church frequently received a substantial dose of Holy Roller ministry.

People called the pentecostals Holy Rollers not because they were separatists but because it was said their worship featured times of emotional bliss during which believers would fall to the floor and roll back and forth in glossolalian ecstasy. In one town, the Holy Roller church held an evangelistic service every Saturday night. High school students frequently attended a meeting for the purpose of a good laugh.

I never did.

Little attention was paid by adults to pentecostal churches because they thought they were only a will-o-the-wisp phenomenon . . . that is none except for the church in the county seat, Carson Lake, which had a fairly large congregation. The other Holy Roller churches in our county consisted of only a dozen to twenty members. Since membership tended to be middle-aged and older, it was simply a matter of a few more funerals and the majority of those churches would be remodeled into low cost residences.

The pastor of the church in the county seat was asked to resign when a woman in the congregation . . . supposedly being counseled by the pastor . . . became pregnant. What complicated the circumstance was the fact her husband was on overseas military duties at the time. Having been on the assignment for several months, he wouldn't be returning until the full year was out.

In spite of his presumed chicanery, the pastor had been doing what was considered by many, to be the work of the Lord with considerable success A few of the members began to have second thoughts, but the die was cast. Nothing could hinder the immediate departure of this spiritually injured servant of the Lord.

Thus came to pass the remarkable demonstration of the Holy Spirit's adroitness in the sacred management of the affairs in the lives of God's children in Carson Lake!

I have told you these things
so that in me you may have peace.
In this world you will have trouble but take heart!
I have overcome the world.
John 16:33

THREE

God's Messenger to Northwest Iowa

The availability of a pentecostal pulpit in Carson Lake, Iowa came to the attention of Dr. J. Whitney Morrison when he was honorably retired at the age of sixty from a prominent and affluent Presbyterian church in Schenectady, New York.

At about this same time he learned through a small advertisement on the church page of the evening Gazette that the well-known theologian, Dr. Charles White, was returning to the area and would be giving lectures on the topic, "The Place of the Holy Spirit in the Lives of Modern Christians." Further, the advertising stated that these lectures would convene in the ballroom of the Schenectady Hotel.

During the concluding years of his ministry, Dr. J, the name his pasrisioners had given him, had come across a book by Dr. Charles White which he was currently reading for the fifth or sixth time! It provided him with information about the Holy Spirit that was almost completely lacking in his seminary training. Further, it had given impetus to his search for pentecostal clergymen in the Schenectady area. The result was a small group of brothers who convened weekly for Tuesday breakfast at the hotel coffee shop. He found the men ideal associates who answered his questions and did not pressure him on other theological subjects.

Dr. J decided to attend Dr. White's opening lecture. He was

surprised but pleased to see members of the Tuesday breakfast group scattered throughout the audience.

On that first night, Dr. White was adlibbing pleasantly with his audience when a woman of obvious means, as indicated by the finery with which she bedecked herself and not excluding the quality and quantity of jewelry she wore, abruptly stood to her feet and began an eloquent uttering of a tongues manifestation.

"When you finish your lecture in that unknown tongue," Dr. White called out, "I will begin my lecture in common English!"

A sizable laugh moved across the audience.

Dr. White had his listeners in hand from the first item of his dissertation. He began, saying, "I presume some of you have heard about the fellow who said he wished he knew where he was going to die. If he knew the place, he'd never go within fifty miles of it as long as he lived." Once again the audience responded with laughter. Dr. J. Whitney Morrison, a man of mirth in his own right, emitted laughter with the same distinction as that of his spoken voice, in this case causing the audience to sustain its jollification until Dr. White raised his hand in pleasant restraint.

Upon Dr. J's arrival for the lecture, an usher had fortuitously placed him near the front directly in the lecturer's line of sight. To be more specific, Dr. White, early in his discourse, selected this affable member of the audience as his contact point by which he could readily determine how well his lecture was being received. For this reason, by the conclusion of the presentation, considerable rapport had developed between the two gentlemen.

Following the lecture, the two ministers were formally introduced. A simple, now forgotten comment caught the attention of Dr. White, and he inquired, "What does that have to do with your interest in the AG . . . that is . . . in the Assemblies of God congregations of this city?"

"It's a long story," Dr. J began pensively. "Do you have about thirty minutes?"

"You've got an eager listener."

He began with his experiences as a young man who, upon completing his college education, enrolled in one of the leading seminaries of his denomination. He had a consuming interest in God, only he wasn't exactly sure whether or not God even existed. The farther he proceeded in seminary studies the more confused he became.

"It got so the congregation of my first parish . . . and my second, and third, and fourth parishes . . . were even more confused than their pastor was," Dr. J admitted to his new friend.

"I happened to meet the pastor of the leading Assemblies of God congregation in the city, and as a result, began attending evening evangelistic services at my new friend's church.

"One Sunday evening, during a series of sermons from Hebrews, his text was the sixth verse of the eleventh chapter. *But without faith it is impossible to please God, because anyone who comes to Him must believe that He exists and that He rewards those who earnestly seek Him.*

"I knew nothing about faith. My pastor friend led me to Romans 10:17: *Faith comes by hearing the message, and the message is heard through the word of Christ."*

"Can you accept it as that?" Dr. White interrupted Dr. J's story.

"I can!" Dr. J exclaimed, new dimensions of understanding and joy coming into his mind and heart.

Leafing through his Bible, Dr. White came to Romans 6:23 and showed it to Dr. J, saying "What about this?"

For the wages of sin is death, but the gift of God is eternal life in Christ Jesus our Lord.

What happened in those next moments was that Dr. J. Whitney Morrison became a believer, a new creation in Christ Jesus (2 Corinthians 5:17).

They talked at length about the Bible, its message, and its claim upon his life. Throughout Dr. White's nightly meetings in Schenectady, the two men rendezvoused in the coffee shop.

On their final evening, Dr. White asked, "Sixty is quite young for a clergyman to retire, isn't it? Would you consider another church of your denomination?"

"No, my retirement is official."

"What about another denomination?"

"A pentecostal church?" Dr. J asked, trying to interpret the twinkle in Dr. White's eyes.

"Would I need to attend one of your seminaries?"

"Ordinarily, yes. You heard me mention the school which I direct?"

Dr. J nodded his head

"We often have pastors join us from other denominations," Dr. White explained. "Sometimes a new pastor can shepherd one of our churches. At the school I direct, we have a one year course of orientation for such pastors. He can take our orientation course by correspondence."

"I should like very much to visit the school!"

A waiter came and filled their cups, and they continued sipping their coffee.

"Have you ever heard of Carson Lake, Iowa?" Dr. White asked.

Dr. J shook his head.

"Each summer I go to Carson Lake. It's a beautiful place in northwest Iowa. There's an old Chautauqua auditorium there, an excellent facility for the type of meeting I present. There is also one of the churches of our denomination which has recently disposed of its pastor and is eagerly in search of another. We had pretty good leadership, but, unfortunately, we had to share it with a man who was also a rapscallion."

Thus, it came to be that Dr. J. Whitney Morrison became the pastor of a pentecostal church in Carson Lake near my home.

The people in the pews were astounded by the new pastor's very first sermon, his eloquence, his depth, his personality.

Through the days of the week, the new preacher spent most of his time on the street. He would greet those he met with a simple, "I am Dr. J. Whitney Morrison, new pastor of the Assembly of God here in Carson Lake." After a few days, he parked himself on one of the benches downtown. At first, people greeted him and then passed by. He had a vast store of jokes, and he began repeating them with the result that he immediately began drawing sizable crowds. More than that, he became the subject of discussion all over town.

One day, when he brought his church announcements into the newspaper office, the editor overheard his voice and came out to ask him if he would submit to an interview. They met in the editor's office, and he did the kind of interview Dr. J recalled from Schenectady.

When the next issue of the paper appeared . . . it was published on Tuesdays and Thursdays . . . an excellently written article appeared on the front page with this headline: "New York Presbyterian Preacher Occupies Pulpit of Carson Lake." The paper stated Dr. Morrison held services on Sunday afternoon to avoid conflict with other churches in the community.

Only the funeral of some local celebrity could have filled the Assembly of God sanctuary as happened the Sunday following this front-page publicity.

Because of the huge crowd, Dr. J announced, "Before I begin my message, I think we would be wise to plan the location of our next

Sunday's meeting place. Until warm weather arrives, do you suppose it would be possible for us to use the high school auditorium on Sunday afternoons?"

People all over the sanctuary spoke up stating that the auditorium was always free on Sundays. The chairman of the school board himself said he could confirm right then its availability, and this would be a public service of the school and there would be no charge.

Dr. J was going to mention the Chautauqua Pavilion, presuming that site would be as readily available as the high school. Since the location for the next Sunday service was arranged, he continued with his sermon.

Some of the people became regulars, attending Sunday afternoon after Sunday afternoon. But then, tactfully, with the guidance of the correspondence school lessons he was doing, Dr. J began to develop sermons around Pentecostal theology, as he was learning to understand it.

This caused some of the people to stop attending. Although others took their place, Dr. J discontinued the use of the high school auditorium and they returned to their sanctuary for the Sunday morning service even as the congregation did expand some. No manifestations of any kind were permitted on Sunday mornings. Sunday evenings, with the church sanctuary comfortably filled, was another matter. Yet, even here, Dr. J emphasized the kind of teaching he had received from Dr. White.

As warm days of spring came, cooperation was as enthusiastic as ever, so he switched the Sunday worship services to the Chautauqua Pavilion. This intensified county-wide curiosity and interest.

Earlier, before the full advent of spring, Dr. White came to visit him, his primary reason being to check arrangements for his summer program. Dr. J arranged for him to occupy the pulpit the Sunday of his visit, and the Chautauqua Pavilion had one of its largest crowds.

When Dr. White arrived for his summer program, he began to bring talent into Carson Lake for Sunday services. Often, he would feature famous performers from as far away as Chicago, bringing them in a few days early to be featured in a special community-wide event. Performers always closed their programs with a couple of hymns.

The Lost Chord, for example, held audiences spellbound.

Often, the visiting celebrities would give their personal witness, affirming that they, too, had found the Master.

By the time summer arrived full-scale, and with it Dr. White's Bible teaching ministry at the Chautauqua Pavilion, Carson Lake was like a little Jerusalem. Dr. White's program convened Sunday afternoons. A smaller group of Carson Lake residents attended those lectures, but the absence of the locals was taken over by those who drove in from out in the county.

Needless to say, the image of Pentecostalism improved measurably in our county as a result of Dr. White's annual summer visits. Through this series of events my heart became thoroughly prepared and eager for the place of the Holy Spirit in my life.

Am I now trying to win the approval of man, or of God?
Or am I trying to please men?
If I were still trying to please men,
I would not be a servant of Christ.
Galatians 1:10

FOUR

On
The
Spot

Several years later, while I was a student at the Northwestern University's Medill School of Journalism, I received an invitation to speak at a Sunday evening service at a Pentecostal church near our home. Learning from a check of our records that this church used our films, especially on Sunday nights, I became all the more anxious to meet the pastor and his people. The pastor seemed a mite nervous when I met him on my arrival.

"You will find our people a discerning group," the pastor said as he led me into his study and gestured for me to sit.

"What I mean by discerning," he continued, " . . . let's put it this way. Discerning Christians wonder why you make your films so biblically dynamic in so many ways, yet you leave out the most important aspects."

I cleared my throat, caught too off-guard to respond.

The pastor stood, looking down at me. Now, it was he who cleared his throat as, sternly like a judge, he asked, "Brother Ken, why don't you present the full Gospel in your films?"

I waited for him to further explain himself.

He didn't.

I made a bold attempt to respond to his statement by saying, "What you see in our films must be acceptable to many different denominations. Some of them have fine-point doctrinal ideas that are different from others. You see. . ."

"Oh, that's what I was afraid of," the pastor interrupted. "The reason you fail to defend the full Gospel is because it wouldn't be good for business, right?"

He continued looking at me, slowly shaking his head like a judge about to pronounce sentence.

"Tell me, Brother Ken," he asked sternly. "When did you receive the baptism of the Holy Ghost? You know . . . praising the Lord in the language of heaven?"

"Well," I stammered. It was as though he had plunged his fist into my stomach.

The sound of the congregation's singing the first evening hymn came now from the sanctuary. The pastor seemed about ready to pounce forward and lay hands upon me but paused a moment instead. With a gesture of his hand, he moved toward the door. I meekly followed.

As we entered the sanctuary, I had the feeling of being an indicted criminal. The audience looked at me as though I were some kind of specimen, the choir a panel of jurors, and the pastor a combination prosecutor and judge.

As the pastor and I entered the sanctuary, his comment about the attitude of the people gave rise to a suspicion in my mind. I wondered if at the morning worship service the pastor had told his people that that night, at the evening service, if they wanted to see spiritual conflict in the Word of God, the church was the place to come.

Did he have something up his charismatic sleeve?

As I told you, I am by nature shy. But I cannot remember so much as a tinge of animosity as I scanned the congregation. They appeared to be good people. Apparently they cared about me to some measure at least. Might this be God's method for dealing with the pride I constantly nurtured in my life as He had often done before?

44

For the evening's text, the pastor, at my request, read from Amos 5:21-27. The first few verses are:

> *I hate, I despise your feast days, and I will not smell in your solemn assemblies. Though you offer me burnt offerings, and your meat offerings I will not accept them; Neither will I regard the peace offering of your fat beasts. Take away from me the noise of your songs; for I will not hear the melody of your vials . . .*

"Well, now," the pastor commented pleasantly after he had read the entire text. "That sounds like an interesting portion of Scripture!" Turning to look back at me, he stated with what appeared to be genuine camaraderie, "We'll be anxious to hear what the Lord has for us through you, Brother Ken."

The song leader led the congregation in one more number following which the pastor stepped to the pulpit to ask another question, "Aren't we pleased to have brother Ken Anderson with us tonight?" he began.

An outburst of applause responded to his inquiry.

He turned back for another glance toward me, saying, "Remember, Brother Ken, I told you our people are really anxious to hear you."

My apprehension intensified.

Returning his attention to the audience, he asked another question.

"How many of you have seen at least one of Ken's films?"

Hands went up all over the auditorium.

The pastor became less amiable now. He stiffened and spoke with effort. "I'm a bit hesitant as to how I should introduce our speaker tonight. I . . . uh . . . regret that the Presbyterian church, as many discerning Christians know, has been occupying itself with the thinking of this world."

The audience grew restless.

"We need to spend much time in prayer for our brothers in the Presbyterian church. You see . . . most . . . uh . . . ." He cleared his throat. "Many of them know nothing about the baptism of the Holy Ghost."

Audience restlessness increased. The pastor stood a moment, mute. Then, glancing back he motioned for me to come to the pulpit which I did as the audience applauded.

"Perhaps you have heard this saying," I introduced. I decided to begin right at the heart of my intended message.

"The New is in the Old contained.

The Old is in the New explained."

Suddenly . . . like a thrust . . . came a loud glossolalia utterance from a woman at the rear of the sanctuary. I tried to continue my message, as though not noticing. The audience seemed as startled as I was. People were looking first at the speaker, then up to the pastor.

I, too, looked at the pastor. Then, looking back toward the audience, as the utterance continued, I saw a woman from the congregation hurry back to the lady and, taking her in a warm embrace, whisper something into her ear. Immediately, the glossolalia ended and the two removed themselves through the back door of the sanctuary.

"Go ahead, Brother Ken!" the pastor called out.

I stumbled on with my message. "The Old Testament believers . . . when they presented their burnt offerings to the Lord . . . believed the smoke from the altar ascended to the very nostrils of Jehovah.

"Okay, Christ . . . the perfect offering for sin . . . lamb with no blemish. . . . Do you see it?"

I had never before that time, and seldom since, shared the

Scriptures with a more responsive and spiritually alert group of Christians.

"Flip over in your Bibles to Ephesians 5:2 in which Paul writes, *Live a life of love, just as Christ loved us and gave himself up for us as a fragrant offering and sacrifice to God.*

"We all know Romans 12:1-2," I said. "Where do we always place the offering?"

"The altar!" called out one man, holding up his Bible.

"Well, okay," I continued, "Do you all agree Romans 12:1-2 refers to placing the sacrifice on the altar?"

"Yes! Yes!" came from all over the congregation.

"All right," I continued. "If Romans 12: 1-2 refers to the altar, what are verses 3-21 of Romans 12?

Some of the people checked their Bibles. Others compared Scriptures with each other.

"Any of you have an idea?"

"Yeah!" one high school boy exclaimed.

"What is it?"

"Romans 12:3-21," he said. "Is . . . that may be the smoke that rises from the sacrifice on the altar."

"Wait a minute!" a girl called out. She came bolting out of her seat, moving toward the boy, stepping on a few toes in doing so. "Look what I found!" she exclaimed, stepping up alongside the boy.

"Look at this, Chuck."

"What you got, Emily?" the boy asked as she stood beside him.

Using her Bible as the reference point, she turned in the boy's Bible.

"You read it, Chuck."

The boy agreed, saying, "Okay, I'll read it. 2 Corinthians 2:14?"

"No, verse 15," Emily corrected.

"Oh, yeah."

"Read it."

Chuck began, "2:15. *For we are to God the aroma of Christ among those who are being saved and those who are perishing.* I see!" Chuck exclaimed.

"See what?" Emily wanted to know.

"Tell us what you are seeing, Chuck," I challenged from the pulpit.

"Okay," Chuck responded, "Take Romans 12:1-2. That's about the altar. It is on the altar that we commit ourselves to God. Right?" he said looking to me for approval.

"You're right so far," I commended. "Go ahead."

"Okay," Chuck continued. "Just like wood on a fire, so our bodies which conformed to the world are transformed. That means they burn in the Holy Spirit's fire."

"So what about verses 3-21?" Emily wanted to know.

"That's the smoke that rises from the altar," Chuck said.

"Sure!" Emily exclaimed. "Listen to this. *'Love must be sincere. Hate that which is evil; cling to what is good.'*"

Chuck took over reading further. "*Be devoted to one another in brotherly love. Honor one another above yourselves.*"

Reading in her Bible again, Emily observed, "See . . . there in Romans 12:1-2 . . . *the transforming fire on the altar.*" She continued reading to herself.

"What fire?" I asked.

"The fire of the Holy Spirit!" Chuck said.

The two young people stood together checking out the Scriptures. Presently, they looked up at me, and Chuck asked, "Did you figure all this out yourself?"

Looking momentarily at the pastor, I said, "I had the Holy Spirit's guidance."

"Wow!" Chuck exclaimed.

"Okay, as it says in the text, *Present your body a living sacrifice, holy, acceptable unto God.* Wasn't it fire on God's altar, too? Verse two: *. . . but be not conformed to this world; but be you transformed by the renewing of your mind."*

I concluded my message, then offered a closing prayer.

The valid rapport I had with those people was obvious.

"See you, Ken," the pastor mumbled evasively. "I have a phone call to make."

"Oh-ee!" sang out one of the parishioners, "I reckon I've been filled with the Holy Spirit a half dozen times, and you'd never find me coming up with that kind of stuff!"

The counselor, the Holy Spirit, whom the Father
will send in my name, will teach you all things. . .

John 14:26

FIVE

Many Facets of Learning

My work has taken me to over one hundred countries, necessitating months away from home. One year it was seven months. You can understand the respect and appreciation I have for my wife and the mother and father roles she shouldered during my absence from home.

We have seven children, each of them guided to faith either by one of their parents or by both of us ministering in tandem. Over the years, most of them have traveled with me to the Singapore assignments. Several have been on productions. Lane joined me in Pakistan to work on *The Living Book* and in Hong Kong to film *To Inhale the Incense.* Margaret and Max were members of the crew for the production of *Mark of the Red Hand* in Bangalore, India, a video drama used around the world in the evangelism of children. Donn and Ken, Jr. spearheaded a production of several filmstrips in guerilla-infested jungles of Colombia, where, on three occasions, murderous partisans moved in directly after we departed from an area. One place they arrived literally on our heels, within a couple of hours after we had taken off on our return flight to Bogota.

But prior to all those encounters, when our children were tots at home with their mother, I went alone to Nairobi, Kenya to join media missionary, Hal Fisher, in the production of *Between Two Worlds*, a motion picture sponsored by the Presbyterian Board of Missions and used by the Holy Spirit to bring many African young people to a personal knowledge of Jesus Christ as their Savior.

As we were sketching out plans for scenes to be shot in a marketplace, a stranger appeared.

"I was wondering if you could use a volunteer," he began pleasantly. "I don't know much about movie making, but I've got a strong back and a willing heart."

"You're hired!" I exclaimed, extending my hand.

Thus began my long and meaningful friendship with Del and Marlys Kingsrighter, Assemblies of God missionaries to East Africa.

It was in Singapore where, along with another American, Joe Weatherly of Youth for Christ, we produced the motion picture, *Something to Die For.* This film was released in a couple hundred prints and has been the means of transforming lives all over the world.

It was during the production of *Something to Die For* that God permitted me to have an experience which often caused me to wonder if I had charismatic inclinations.

We'd had a hard week filming in the equatorial heat of Singapore, and when Sunday morning came we worshiped at a Brethren assembly. After service, we quickly returned to our base at Youth for Christ Headquarters. Tom Spaulding and Godfrey Buss, producers of the motion picture, *The Blob*, were checking footage in the air-conditioned YFC office. My cousin, Dean Sundblad, and I turned on a couple of ceiling fans and were soon asleep.

Suddenly, I awakened and sat up on the cot. Across my mind, almost as though I heard them spoken, came the words, "My wife needs me, and I can't do a thing to help her!"

From that moment, I came full awake, smitten, as I often had been, by what I call *geographical claustrophobia.* This is a concept which cannot be explained, only experienced, when you realize how inescapably separated you are from your family and ministry at home.

My cousin awakened, and I shared the thoughts with him.

We prayed together. It was good for my spirits.

Shortly after we prayed, and as we sat chatting for a few moments, we heard the sound of a scooter, the familiar audio trademark of young fellows who delivered cables in Singapore. I got to my feet to check. Tom and Godfrey had stepped outside the door.

"That cable's for me!" I cried out, so sure something having gone awry for my wife back home.

"Are you Mr. Anderson?" the cable boy asked.

I showed him my passport. He handed me the envelope. I opened the cable, motioning for my cousin to look with me. Together we read my wife's message. It said simply:

"My dad died this afternoon."

Later, I learned that Grandpa Jones had gone to a showing of our film, *That Kid Buck.* Several young people had responded to the invitation.

A sincere Christian, my wife's father rejoiced seeing the young converts, and then he dropped dead.

A lady kneeling beside him, noting the dead man's faith as evidenced by his Gideon pin, exclaimed, "He got to heaven just in time to hear the angels rejoicing!"

Back now to Del Kingsrighter.

It was Del who, years later, drove me from Nairobi, Kenya, to Entebbe, Uganda, to investigate possibilities for a documentary film on the evil madman and dictator, Idi Amin.

Ever the enterpriser, Del had already established the acquaintance of a Tanzanian lieutenant who told him he had access to most of the strategic sites related to the infamous doings of Amin.

A month earlier, Tanzanian troops had crossed Lake Victoria like an invading armada and, storming ashore, frightened Ugandan soldiers so intensely, they threw down their guns and ran for cover. Idi Amin himself took off in one of the government airplanes to save his neck.

During the writing of this chapter in mid-August of 2003, Idi Amin, who had taken shelter in Saudi Arabia, died of syphilis and gonorrhea.

Del had told a Tanzanian army officer about our plans for possibly doing a documentary film, and the lieutenant urged Del to check with him for keys to get into special buildings. One of the keys supplied by the lieutenant opened the door to the building containing the horror chambers where Idi Amin had held many of his special prisoners, including Archbishop Luwuum, who was murdered by Amin himself.

The first level had window lights which let in sufficient illumination to give us a good view of the area. This, we would later learn, was where Idi Amin would bring some of his older sons to watch as the prisoners were brought up from the chambers below and compelled to fight each other to the death.

Prowling the infamous death chambers, the upper level illuminated by sparse daylight, we came upon a pile of booklet tracts, hundreds, more likely thousands of them, titled *Help From Above.* They had been published and distributed by World Missionary Press with headquarters a scant nine miles from my home in Indiana.

Beyond the pile of booklets a staircase led down into utter darkness.

"It never entered my mind to bring a flashlight," Del lamented.

His face suddenly brightened. He thrust his hand into one of his jacket pockets, as he exclaimed, "Oh, here's a couple of match folders I picked up in a hotel someplace!"

He began moving cautiously down the stairway toward the darkness. I followed. As Del entered the dark area, he struck one match. With its illumination, we ventured into a large cell block.

The lower area was comprised entirely of these cell blocks, each large enough to hold a group of prisoners.

"Hundreds of people were jammed into each of these cells," Del explained. "They had to sleep in shifts as it was impossible for all the prisoners to lie down at one time."

The matches from the first folder got us into the deepest area, a large room which would probably hold about fifty people, but into which, we later learned, two hundred were jam-packed.

"Here, let's try something." Del said bringing out the final match folder. He spread the matches then carefully ignited them so they all burned at once for a few moments.

"Hold it closer to the floor," I said.

Del complied.

Then, with my foot, I scraped the mud-like surface of the floor.

"Do you know what that is?" Del queried.

"Dried human blood!" I gasped.

Then, by the dying light of Del's match folder, we stumbled our way back to the staircase and up into the daylight.

We made little comment, either of us, during the several hours drive back to Nairobi.

Del's wife, Marlys, had a tasty evening meal awaiting.

I only dabbled with my food, apologizing profusely to Marlys for my scant appetite.

Del explained to his lady some of the things we had witnessed, especially in the horror chambers, and she too began dawdling with her food.

The fireplace logs that Del had set ablaze prior to the meal time now rid the house of late mountain chill and added a bright flickering background to the candles.

"Some missionaries," Del began, "especially those new to the field, have actually scolded us for having such a classy lifestyle."

"Hold it! Hold it!" I rebutted. "I've stayed in the homes of many wealthy American expatriates which couldn't touch the charm of your place. Why? Because they couldn't touch Marlys's simplistic expertise."

Marlys chuckled at the statement of her "simplistic expertise" and resumed her listening stance.

"Well," I continued. "Look at us now. A cozy fireside with a half dozen candles. Perfect therapy after those haunting minutes we spent in the horror chambers today."

Our conversation wandered to other personal matters. Our families . . . our churches.

I missed our presbytery back home in Indiana . . . the lay people I knew who had spiritual sensitivities rare in the Body of Christ those days. "Lots of Presbyterians," I said, "are seeking more of the Holy Spirit. Actually, I occasionally meet a few, only a few it would seem . . . but there are those who are exploring the charismatic movement . . . even within their church." I told Marlys and Del about my own personal experience seeking the Holy Spirit's fullness in my life.

Del stoked the fire.

Marlys fixed some popcorn which we shared out of a common bowl. On and on into the night we talked. Two more times Del stoked the fire. One by one, candles of varying length burned to their base. Marlys was going to replace them, but we all agreed a varying intensity of light added an intrigue to the setting and to our discussion.

It became as natural as breathing for me to mention the church where I had been bluntly confronted by my apparent lack of maturing experiences with the Holy Spirit.

"Was it one of our churches?" Marlys asked, a hint of anxiety in her voice.

I remembered the pastor having told me his church was an

independent member of a charismatic fellowship but of no denomination.

Spirited!

That word described our conversation much of the evening. At times, however, we quieted down. Maybe for five minutes or so we just enjoyed a couple handfuls of popcorn.

Shortly after a distant mantel clock had struck the hour of two, Del gave a self-awakening snort.

"Does that mean time to get up or go to bed?" Marlys asked.

Both of them looked at me.

"I didn't come here to sleep. I came here to pick your brains and your hearts."

"How about a potty break?" Del asked.

The three of us got to our feet. "There's a facility just off of the kitchen," Del said.

"Off the kitchen? It's illegal in LA," I replied.

"This ain't LA! There's another one upstairs," he announced.

I headed up there.

Within twenty minutes we were all at hearth's side, each with a cup of hot chocolate embellished with marshmallows plus a communal supply of dunking materials.

The two of them wanted to know more about Presbyterians who were interested in Pentecostalism.

I shared an example. The only one that came to my mind at the moment and was not very flattering.

Two or three of the top men in our town . . . all Presbyterians . . . became involved in the extreme doctrines of a fringe pentecostal group. Believing strongly in divine healing, one family refused medication for their children who had become ill. The end result was that the children died.

Finally, after a short pause, we held hands and each offered a brief prayer, then retired.

I fell asleep thanking God for the encounter I was having with these two choice people. Also, more sincerely than anything I had ever done before, I asked God not to withhold from me anything He wanted me to have.

I awakened early the next morning, dressed, and went downstairs. To my surprise, I came upon Del pacing in the living room where we had had such a meaningful time a few hours previous.

"Marlys and I couldn't fall asleep till almost daybreak," he said. "We talked and talked to see how to categorize somebody like you."

"Did you decide?" I asked.

"Yes, we did."

From across the interior of the house in the kitchen came the chimes on the mantel clock announcing 7:00 a.m. Immediately following that, Marlys rang the breakfast bell. Del led the way to the dinette where Marlys appeared with some tasty choices for the morning meal.

"What did you decide?" I asked again.

Del slipped over beside his wife. They stood together, arm in arm, and Del said, "We decided you're just as charismatic as we are!"

I appeal to you brothers,
in the name of the Lord Jesus Christ,
that all of you agree with one another
so that there be no division among you
and that you be perfectly united in mind and thought.
I Corinthians 1:10

Six

Martyrs
And My
Pride
Syndrome

Things were looking good for Ken Anderson!

Zondervan became a publishing phenomenon. Ted Engstrom, named managing editor of the thriving enterprise, became as much my agent as he was editor of the publishing house and remained a close friend beyond a half century and on into the 21st century. Twice annually, Ted and the two Z brothers, Bernie and Pat, summoned me to the mezzanine lobby of the Pantland Hotel in Grand Rapids where we laid out my next year of writing assignments.

That same hotel became the site of Zondervan's quarter century celebration. I was honored as the Zondervan Youth Books Author of the Quarter Century. Subsequently, the Evangelical Press Association named me Feature Writer of the Year. For an Iowa farm boy, this was really big time!

In retrospect, I realize how sorely afflicted I had become with spiritual pride. At the time, however, I reveled in the glory of feeling that I had been singularly anointed by the Holy Spirit for exalted duty as a dispenser of the Word through writing.

I wonder now why God didn't strike me dead for such effrontery.

As editor of the Youth for Christ Magazine, I began receiving many invitations to speak at Youth for Christ rallies. Almost every

Saturday night I was somewhere, usually overnight sleeper train distance from Chicago. I would remain on Sunday and return Sunday night to be in Chicago first thing Monday morning.

The weekend appointments involved some of the largest churches in North America. For example, I spoke one Sunday morning and Sunday evening at People's Church in Toronto. I held a week of children's meetings in the main auditorium of the Moody Church in Chicago.

I should rise above my ego to point out that most of these rallies and appointments came as the result of my going as a substitute. Billy Graham began with the YFC organization as its first full-time evangelist and became instantly popular. Booked for a rally in a smaller place, he would receive and accept an urgent call from one of the large rallies. Torry Johnson would call me into his office and tell me I was to go to the smaller rally as a substitute for Billy Graham. Somehow swallowing my pride, I learned to live with it. I was often loathed by the rally directors who saw me get off the train or the airplane instead of Billy Graham. I realized belatedly that pride is a powerful barrier to spiritual progress.

With the development of Gospel Films, my options for overseas activity, which is my prime interest, increased. It was then that I began to discover some true but extremely agonizing stories of valid Christian heroes.

Martyrs!

Few people living in the United States knew much more about martyrs than the definition in the Oxford Dictionary which states, *One who voluntarily undergoes the penalty of death by refusing to renounce the Christian faith.* It was academic for me. I knew that during the middle decades of the twentieth century, China provided an abundance of modes of martyrdom, and it was not the only nation creating martyrs. But with the religious freedoms I experienced in the

United States, martyrs had nothing to do with me . . . or so I thought.

One time I was in India with Dr. Geoffrey Lehmann who financed many of our productions. I told him of my interest in doing a film on Sadhu Sundar Singh, far and away India's most famous Christian. "I would be pleased to verify with my charitable trust in England to determine if the film is within our capability at this time," said Geoffrey. We discussed the cost, and it was clearly within the doctor's financial capability.

We had the option of using one of India's super cinema stars who had won the Indian equivalent of the Oscar a half dozen times. When I visited him on the set in Bombay, it was plain to see that this man truly loved stardom. He was a Presbyterian, which interested me some, but the more time I spent with him the more I realized he was typical of many Indians those days. He worshiped Jesus, but I am not at all sure if he really knew Jesus.

"He takes a lot of watching," one young producer cautioned me. "I directed him in a feature a couple of years back, and I finally had to accept the fact that whenever he had a highly dramatic scene to do, he always arrived on set drunk as a hog. He is a full-time womanizer, as well."

I became very concerned and began asking God to send us the right actor for this important role. Then one night, as Dr. Lehman and I sat talking about our problem, there was a knock on the door.

It was a young Hindu, apparently a man of much wealth, who had heard about our looking for an actor to play the part of Sadhu Sundar Singh. He told us the thrilling story of how he had picked up a Bible at a bazaar and upon reading it became a believer.

"Have you ever done any acting?" I asked. Hearing my question, he brightened and told us one of his majors at the university had been drama.

He had been especially intrigued with the fact we were planning to do a film on the life of Sadhu Sundar Singh.

"Since I became a Christian," he told us "I have been very interested in the Sadhu. I have read several books about him."

I asked if he could stay with us for a few days and help me work on the script.

This interested him very much, but as he thought a moment, he sobered.

"I must go home and tell my father and my brothers that I have become a Christian. It will take a couple of days, and then I will come back."

His parental home was in Dehra Dun, a short distance beyond Dr. Lehman's hospital. I tried to get his address, but for some reason he didn't want to give it to me.

"By the end of next week," I told him, "we must begin production so that I can return to America."

"Oh," he assured me, "I'll return early next week at the latest." Then he left.

Actually, I waited several days longer than planned, urgently desiring to spend some time with him.

Finally, we contracted the famous actor.

On the last day of production just before I left for home, a Hindu friend of the doctor's came to the hospital. He seemed quite troubled. He mentioned the name of the young man who had come to see us but had never returned as promised.

"You know him?" the doctor exclaimed.

"I did," the young man replied. "You must not have heard what happened to him."

Then, as the doctor and I listened awestruck, the visitor told us of this young man. He had returned to his family and told them of his conversion.

His father, one of Dehra Dun's most prominent Hindu leaders, demanded his son recant. This he refused, so his brothers stoned him to death. Because of the father's prominence, they had no difficulty fabricating the death certificate to state that the martyr had died of natural causes.

"That is another to add to our list of martyrs here at the hospital," said the doctor. Whereupon he cited a number of similar stories about converts who had become martyrs at the hands of their family rather than reject their faith.

Some have been allowed to avoid martyrdom but have been left to endure intense suffering. One example shared by Dr. Lehman is recorded in the next chapter, *Facing Martyrdom.*

One day when I was back in my office in the United States, I received a telephone call from Bob Pierce who like Billy Graham, was an evangelist-at-large with Youth for Christ. The previous summer, Bob had gone to China and had an amazing reception. He requested I go with him the following summer to do some writing primarily for our magazine and possibly also a book. His highest priority was the need for a documentary motion picture that told the story of China's suffering.

"Mao Tse Tung will have China under his control within the year," Bob Pierce told me. "He will have the Nationalist Army groveling in defeat. China is becoming a land of martyrs, Ken, and we've got to tell the world about it."

Our last airport before China was Tokyo. I can never forget the terrifying air view of that huge city. It looked like a gigantic honeycomb. American and British pilots had dropped incendiary bombs destroying thousands of homes and buildings leaving only the stone foundations.

Several hours beyond Tokyo, the Pan Am captain himself came back to tell us that in a few minutes we would be flying over Hiroshima. A strange chill came over me as I looked down at Hiroshima ground zero. It looked as though a giant's hand had reached down and scooped up vast areas of the city.

Bob Pierce put an arm across my shoulder and whispered, "Buddy, look at it! Tens of thousands of people are dying . . . most of them dying for nothing. Let's trust God that when we die, we will have at least died for something!"

Entering Shanghai, our first port of call in China, was one of the most traumatic experiences of my entire life. The city was a nightmare of traffic congestion. One hundred bicycles to one automobile, plus masses of people. The moment your vehicle came to a halt, dozens of people with gaunt, hungry countenances surrounded your car pleading for money to buy food.

In those heartbreaking moments, I once again experienced what I've come to call *geographical claustrophobia.* For myself, I also experienced in those moments a cruel reality. I began to face the fact of how much my faith had become a matter of material security. Success for Christians was so often equated with financial stability. A deep conviction began coming over me. It was as though I were a condemned man in prison waiting to face a jury and judge who would find me guilty as charged of the awful sin of making the things of the world my highest priority.

What thoughts went through the minds of these people who had nothing? Okay, so Confucius is the big brain here in China, setting a pattern of thinking and values which has controlled their society for over 2,500 years.

In the Pan Am reader's magazine, I had run across this nugget from the great K'ung Fu-tzu, Chinese philosopher.

"To be able under all circumstances to practice five things constitutes perfect virtue; these five things are gravity, generosity of soul, sincerity, earnestness, and kindness."

Am I supposed to believe that somebody out there in that mass of people is pondering the wisdom of this ancient sage? Most seemed more concerned with surviving at any cost until next week.

"Lord," I prayed in exclaiming silence, "Help me! I don't know how to figure these terrible circumstances."

Then, it came to me so distinctly as I formed my words of intercession.

"Oh, Lord, I know you sent me here to teach me something. Make me a good learner. Change my motives, my attitudes, my sensitivities. Please, oh God, *work me over*!"

God heard my cry and the Holy Spirit graciously ministered to me as China taught me the reality of martyrdom. The Holy Spirit proved to be the all-sustaining Comforter Christ had promised.

During our time in China, we met people whose family members had been buried alive for boldly defying a communist command to renounce their Christian faith. A school teacher was dragged by the hair behind a jeep until she bled to death, the reason being her refusal to substitute Communist-approved textbooks for her traditional variety.

Two brothers told us of the circumstances involved in the death of their father, a godly self-taught expert in Bible exposition.

He was crucified.

Instead of bothering to build a wooden cross, however, the Communists knocked him to the ground, then tore away the outer flesh of his hands and feet with grappling hooks. They then stretched him out in the form of a cross and staked his arms and legs to the ground.

The two brothers watched as their father, just outside their home, tossed and turned in his agony, quoting Bible verses that had special meaning to him.

Finally, when they could bear the sight no longer, the eldest of the two ran to the prone crucifix and knelt beside his suffering father.

"Have mercy," he pled.

The sentry pointed his gun at the saintly old man's head and pulled the trigger.

I was learning the cost of being a follower of Christ. Truly, the Holy Spirit was working in me and revealing my need for new depths of commitment. Am I ready for that?

For it has been granted to you on behalf of Christ
not only to believe on Him, but also to suffer for him.
Philippians 1:29

SEVEN

Facing Martyrdom

"One of the most interesting cases that has come to our hospital," Dr. Lehmann, the English physician in India told us, "is not yet a martyr. He still lives." Then he told me about a young man who had come to the hospital for treatment, and hearing the message of the Gospel, he placed his faith in Jesus Christ. He returned to his home and boldly told his parents. He was a favorite child of the father, and so at first his father begged his son to have pity.

"I cannot have a son who becomes a Christian," the father pleaded. "I suppose I can't ask you to give up your new religion, but I want your promise that you will never speak of it in our community or to anyone who knows us."

The young man tried to be careful, but people began to ask him questions about the change in his life. At first he kept quiet, but his conscience troubled him greatly. So, little by little, he began to witness.

"Would you go spit in your father's face?" asked the oldest brother.

The new convert loved his father very much. He began asking God not to expect him to witness to anyone known by his family.

But it was no use. The new convert had to witness to anyone who would listen.

The brothers tried to persuade their father to kick the insult of the family out of the home, and the news spread all over Dehra Dun. Most Hindus made a joke of him. It really didn't matter. The young man witnessed to them as much as to others.

Hindu leaders came to the father and demanded him to keep his son quiet. They even advised him to destroy his son.

That was a difficult request! He had already asked his son to refrain from sharing his new religion, but that had not stopped him. He knew exactly what he was expected to do, but the thought of killing the son whom he dearly loved was heart-rending.

Then the oldest brother came up with an idea.

"We can quiet him. We don't need to kill him."

Without asking for details, the father reluctantly agreed they could do whatever they decided. Telling his sons he was going to the home of a relative, he left them to their evil plans.

Their decision was to heat a container of oil to hottest pitch. Then, holding their younger brother, they poured the boiling oil into his mouth. In one act of mercy, they took their brother to Dr. Lehmann's hospital.

"He almost died," the doctor related. "But we were able to nurse him back to reasonable health. The boiling oil had destroyed his vocal chords, leaving him mute."

The young Christian became more famous than ever. After months of patient practice, he learned to whisper words audibly and became known as *The Whispering Evangelist.*

I was smitten by that young man's story, and the very thought of it would cause me to think about my own condition, the terrible scourge of my own vanity.

Once, during the earlier part of our stay in China, we were guests in Tientsin, as the city of Tianjin at that time was called, in the home of Mr. and Mrs. Jonathan Lee. Tientsin was known as the Pittsburgh of China. It was also known as a city of millionaires, Jonathan

Lee being one of them. Mr. Lee, a successful exporter, was even more successful as a Christian witness. Together with his wife, he spent most of every day out on the streets preaching the Gospel.

One evening, I asked him when he and his wife would be leaving China.

"Leaving?" Mr. Lee questioned. "Why would we leave?"

Even as we spoke, I could hear the roar of planes overhead. As we both well knew, they were laden with refugees flying either to Hong Kong or to Taipei.

Many of those refugees had scraped together, from the sale of everything they owned, scarcely sufficient funds to purchase one passage on an escaping aircraft.

Note I said "One."

Wife and children would remain behind to accept whatever lot may befall them. We heard of numerous cases where a father literally sold all of his daughters in order to ensure the required price of his own passage.

As both of us also knew, Mr. Lee could purchase one of those planes for his family alone to make their escape.

At that moment, some five thousand Chinese troops were bivouacked ten miles out from the city. There were some five hundred U.S. Marines in Tientsin. As news of Mao Tse Tung's Long March emphasized the rapid capitulation of the Nationalist army, those U.S. Marines prepared to exit Tientsin within 24 hours' notice.

"Surely, Jonathan," I chided, "You don't expect me to believe you would literally stay in this doomed city when it collapses to Mao?"

By the flash in his eyes, I could see that Jonathan Lee was a quick-tempered man. He drew a breath, then came into the full control of his emotions.

In answer to my question as to when he and his family would be leaving China, he spoke with selected, incisive words.

"We could leave China," he said. "We have taken care of our family matters. The Lord has blessed us with a large family and many of our older children are attending school in Hong Kong. Six months ago we also sent the *amahs* with the younger children."

"But you will not leave?" I asked. "That's suicide!"

Jonathan remained intensely serious for a moment. Then a smile slowly brightened his countenance. He reached for a Bible. I could see he turned the pages to the twenty-first chapter of Acts.

Presently he said, "When those who gave the same advice to Paul as you are giving to me, this was Paul's reply: *What are you doing, weeping and breaking my heart? For I am ready not only to be bound, but also to die at Jerusalem for the name of the Lord Jesus. The will of the Lord be done!*"

"So are you challenging God?" I inquired.

"What do you mean?" he asked.

"Do you think God will miraculously spare you when the Communists overtake Tientsin?"

"It is our staying here that will validate the sincerity of our message. When we preach to people these days," he explained, "They say, 'Oh, yes, Mr. Lee wants us to become converts so we can be among the first to die when the Communists take over . . . Die while Mr. and Mrs. Lee are in Taiwan or perhaps Hong Kong enjoying themselves.'"

He sat for a long and quiet moment, gripping his Bible. Then he said, "One day you will hear that Tientsin has fallen. That will open for us the greatest door of spiritual harvest. When people realize we have stayed beyond the opportunity for us to escape, then they will know we are sincere in our witness to them. Then we will be able to win many more to our Savior."

There would be no hope for living if they remained. Staying in place waiting for inevitable martyrdom defied my human logic. The normal survival instinct surpassed by a desire to be a faithful Christian witness was an unimaginable challenge for me.

> *We say with confidence,*
> *'The Lord is my helper; I will not be afraid.*
> *What can man do to me?'*
> Hebrews 13:6

A few weeks later I read in the Chicago Daily News that Tientsin had fallen.

Eight

The Holy Spirit At Work

In numerous major cities of China, we announced evening Youth for Christ rallies at a conveniently located school or church compound.

In Beijing, which was then still known by its old China name, Peking, we used a circus ground as our venue. The very first night, we had at least five thousand students in attendance. Within the week, this grew to more than ten thousand nightly.

We were told it was a common thing to hear young people on a school campus talking about their plans to attend the YFC rally that night for the specific purpose of becoming believers.

I can still remember the choruses they sang and the enthusiasm with which they sang them.

> *Lai sen Jesu, lai sen Jesu, lai sen Jesu xian zai*
> *Xian zai lai sen Jesu, lai sen Jesu xian zai.*

The translation into English produced this simple thought,

> Come to Jesus, come to Jesus, come to Jesus just now,
> Just now come to Jesus, come to Jesus just now.

Many of these choruses were simply translations of English that I had often heard at YFC rallies when I spoke in the States. This heightened the intrigue as I now listened to Chinese kids sing with identical enthusiasm half a world away from Chicago, Los Angeles,

Des Moines or Paducah.

The most memorable of all were the invitations at the conclusion of each message. They were much like Billy and Franklin Graham's invitations. Frankly, they astounded me. A third to a half of the audience would respond. Where are these young people now? Many of them, I presume, make up the enormous house church movement all over China.

I remember writing home and reporting to my wife what we were seeing. She, in turn, would write back warning me to be careful of exaggeration.

Especially in Beijing, the response was so voluminous it began to be a logistical problem. So we decided to change the method. We did not ask the young people to come forward, following the Grahams' procedure, the simple reason being that we could not handle the volume. Instead, we asked the young people who truly wanted to receive Christ as their Savior to return the following night for a meeting time.

You can't guess what happened. On the first attempt at this procedure, all returned the following night as arranged. We estimated over two thousand young people had responded the previous night. And apparently, during the day following, the young people had shared with their friends what they intended to do. And so, when the two thousand young people came for counseling, an equal number of their friends came with them. We had four thousand "seekers," but only a few dozen counselors.

The power of the Holy Spirit was surely in evidence. Christ's promise that *"He (the Holy Spirit) will bear witness of me,"* was being fulfilled before my eyes. At service after service, Christ was lifted up as Savior of the world, and the Holy Spirit was confirming that in the hearts and minds of the listeners. They responded en masse to pray the sinner's prayer.

We not only had these huge youth meetings at night, but we also went to high schools and college campuses during the day. In some of these instances, we were not permitted to make a public invitation. We were, however, allowed to designate a rendezvous point later in the day and throngs of young people would always be there at the announced time so they could confirm their decision to receive Christ as their Savior. We also had Sunday afternoon rallies in churches.

I cannot remember the name of the moderate-sized city in which I was assigned to speak one Sunday morning in the Methodist church. I stayed at a private home, and when it came time to go to the church for the morning service, my host took me to the front of the house and, at random, summoned a rickshaw boy to take me to my destination.

I detested riding in rickshaws, being pulled around like a big shot by another human being. Someone told me that the average life of a rickshaw boy was seven to twelve years. Whenever I rode in a rickshaw in a place where there were hills, I would summon the boy to stop as the rickshaw reached the base of a hill. Then I got out and walked with him to the top of the hill. Occasionally, the rickshaw boy refused to proceed without me in his vehicle, but many more times I received smiles and a sincere *xie xie* for my consideration.

Anyway, my rickshaw boy that Sunday morning lit up with a big smile for a different reason. He saw the Bible I was carrying! He put his finger on it and pointed to himself and rattled off something in Chinese. My runner could speak no English. I could speak no Chinese.

Rickshaw boys were always expected to break off into a trot, and this bothered me. I'd rather arrive at an assignment late and permit the rickshaw boy to walk rather than have him run with me the whole distance.

This rickshaw boy ran the rest of the way, and I got the distinct impression that it was a performance of joy on his part.

When we reached the Methodist church, he seemed hardly to have broken into a sweat.

Across the front of the church was a very large sign. I could make out the letters YFC and the names of Bob Pierce and myself.

The rickshaw boy wanted to know what my name was, so we walked over together to the sign. I pointed to Ken Anderson . . . pronouncing it in English . . . so he could make an effort to say it. He did quite well. In a moment, the pastor came out and met me. He spoke briefly to the rickshaw boy who pointed repeatedly at my Bible as he chattered.

"He said he plans to come to the meeting this afternoon," the pastor said. "He, too, is a Christian."

"Tell him," I said, my voice choked a bit, "that I am honored to have had him pull me to church this morning."

By the time I arrived back at the church for the afternoon rally, I had forgotten about the rickshaw boy. The church was packed with masses of people sitting on the floor.

We had just begun singing the first song when, to my amazement, down from the back entrance of the sanctuary came my new friend, the rickshaw boy, and a half dozen other rickshaw boys. They sat down on the floor just below the pulpit.

Our eyes met.

There were tears in mine at this point!

Bob Pierce was the speaker that afternoon. He told the simple story of a little boy who stole a watermelon and invited some of his friends to share it with him. Then, afraid of being caught, he covered over the scene of his dishonesty.

When his father asked the little boy about the watermelon he had brought home for the family, he wanted to know how much his son knew about it. The boy denied knowing anything.

He forgot all about it, too.

Then one day, when the little boy came home from school, his father asked him to come and see something. The two of them walked a short distance to the spot where the little boy and his friends had eaten most of the melon and then covered over the evidence of the wrongdoing.

"When you covered over the seeds," the father said, "you thought you were hiding the truth of what really happened."

What had actually occurred, of course, was that tiny watermelon plants sprung up wherever seeds had fallen.

At the conclusion of his sermon, Bob Pierce read the Bible verse which warns that you can ". . .be sure your sin will find you out." (Numbers 32:23). Then he asked the audience, "Do you have sin in your life you wish God would forgive? He will!"

Then, he gave an invitation for anyone who wanted to learn how to have his sins forgiven to go out a side door of the sanctuary to a point where a large tent had been erected for counselors and "seekers."

Up to his feet bounded the rickshaw boy and motioning to his friends, he led the way out to the counseling tent. I saw again the Holy Spirit at work. Christ said, *"He (the Holy Spirit) will convict the world concerning sin, and righteousness, and judgment."* I could never be the same after experiencing such a vivid manifestation of conviction and such a spontaneous response.

China was slowly but surely getting its message across to a proud upstart writer by the name of Ken Anderson.

In those days, there was much confusion on the part of the Nationalists who were determined to keep China free. The revolutionary invaders were methodically driving the forces of Generalissimo Chiang Kai Shek into oblivion.

Bob Pierce and I got to know several of the top government officials. One of the cabinet members became quite a good friend of mine. He was China's Surgeon General, a warm Christian, who insisted it was all a matter of strategy.

"The Generalissimo," he said, "is making a fool out of Mao Tse Tung by cunningly enticing him out of the north and down into the heart of Old Cathay. Meanwhile, China's great friend, the United States of America, waits poised for the kill. At precisely the correct moment, the Americans will come storming across China, their tanks covering the ground and their airplanes darkening the sky. In a few short days, they will utterly destroy the unfaithful troops who have been so cleverly hypnotized by the master strategist, Chou En-lai."

How different was his vision from reality!

I must tell you about a girl named Nancy, the four year-old daughter of a missionary couple, who spent the early years of her life in a small, ancient walled city deep in the heart of China. The Chinese Nationalist Army set up a strong military outpost in this little city. As Mao's Long March continued successfully through the interior of the great nation, they inevitably reached this colorful little community.

During the days while she and her family lived in the walled city, a strange phenomenon was taking place. Even though the Nationalist and Communist troops were in close proximity to each other across China, there was little fighting. I heard reports of soldiers from the two armies meeting each other casually and having a hilarious time telling stories of their personal experiences.

Supply trucks from each army would pull up to the same *go-down*, and while their trucks were being filled with supplies, the truck drivers, military men, socialized like old friends.

Initially, when the Long March forces entered an area, the Nationalist troops retreated. Then, seemingly almost without effort, the Nationalists would drive the enemy back north from where they had come.

As previously stated, the small walled city where Nancy's family had its base of operations was a heavily-entrenched Nationalist military citadel. But as Mao's troops arrived, they pre-arranged with the

Nationalists for a takeover. Then, at night while the little city slept the Nationalists left, and Mao Tse Tung's forces took over without firing a shot. As the inhabitants awakened the following morning, they were stunned to see enemy flags had replaced the Nationalist ensigns.

From new entrenchments outside the walls, Nationalist artillery began firing shells into the city.

It so happened that Nancy's home had been built high up against the wall, so that the upstairs windows jutted plainly visible above the ancient barrier. Nancy and her brothers and sisters enjoyed playing in the upstairs room whose windows looked out upon the surrounding countryside. Now, with the Nationalist troops having been expelled, the parents still did not object to the children spending most of their playing time upstairs.

Then, one moonless night, the two enemies reached some kind of accommodation whereby Mao's soldiers slipped silently out of the city. When morning came, Nationalist flags were back as they had been previously.

With the full light of day, enemy artillery began firing shells into the city causing considerable panic across the community.

Nancy's mother demanded they no longer play upstairs. Instead, in a place downstairs deemed as safe, they huddled and began playing a strange game. As each shell was fired and went piercing its way through the air, a peculiar sound designated its direction of origin and the place where it would strike a hard surface and explode on contact.

They became quite proficient at predicting the area of each shell's origin and subsequent impact.

As days passed, and Mao's military was unable to get back into the city, family confidence thrived. They presumed the Communists would simply tire of their unrewarded effort to regain the city and move on in a different direction from which they had come.

Again, Nancy begged for permission to go back to the upstairs bedroom. Since all shells were falling a distance from the house, the parents reluctantly agreed. Gathering at the windows, they watched Communist troops digging into their new positions.

This was the way it had been the last several months. The Communists held the city for a while, then the Nationalists were routing them out and holding the upper hand.

One day the parents, who were disturbed to hear so many Communists' shells being fired, demanded the children remain downstairs with them.

Two days passed. Shells from the Communist artillery units continued their errands of death.

"There aren't any shells falling in our part of the city," Nancy eventually reasoned. "May we please go back upstairs and play again, just for a little while?"

Reluctantly, the parents again agreed.

The children became so engrossed in playing they paid no attention at all to the warfare outside. But then came the whine of another shell. It sounded different from any they had previously heard. The reason? It was heading directly at the upstairs part of the house!

Downstairs, the missionary mother screamed!

Too late, however, as in that instant the shell came crashing through the windows and into the room.

It was the kind of artillery shell that detonated on contact, except that, by the goodness of the Lord, this shell was a dud. Instead of exploding, it crashed through the window in the outside wall, sailed through the room, threading its way among the children like a needle. Then, a larger crash! It passed through the opposite wall and outside beyond the missionary's property.

The parents ran up the stairs to the room where the children stood in mute astonishment.

That evening, when the family gathered for their nightly Bible reading, Nancy said quietly to her father, "Daddy, can we read the story of Daniel in the lion's den?"

"Good idea!" her father approved.

After he had finished, Nancy asked, "We will see Mr. Daniel in Heaven, won't we?"

"We surely will!" her father shared.

"I'm going to go right up to him," she continued, "and ask him to tell me his story of how he felt when he was sure the lions were going to kill him and how wonderful it was when the angels came and saved his life. After Mr. Daniel tells me his story, I'm going to ask if he would like to hear our story!" She fully understood God's protective power.

I need to share with you one more China anecdote.

I was scheduled one morning to lead a Bible study in the home of one of the pastors. I arrived thirty minutes ahead of the others and found myself in the home of a congenial gentleman who could speak barely three words of English. Those words were, "Praising the Lord!"

He motioned for me to sit down for a cup of tea, and as he prepared my serving, he smiled warmly and exclaimed, "Praising the Lord!" Though the number of English words were limited, those three words communicated volumes that only fellow Christians could comprehend. We were one in the Spirit.

"Praising the Lord!" I replied spontaneously.

He pointed to my Bible and said, "Praising the Lord!"

"Praising the Lord!" I echoed. This was my expression indicating we were one in Christ.

He opened his Bible, I opened mine, finding John 3:16. We placed our Bibles side-by-side, the Pinyin and the English.

"Praising the Lord!" was his rollicking comment.

"Praising the Lord!" was also mine.

Although each of us was reading the scripture in our own

language, it seemed as if the Holy Spirit was interpreting what each of us were longing to share with the other.

We had a wonderful time together. He showed me a picture of his family, after which I took out my billfold and withdrew a picture of my wife and me.

"*Tai tai?*" he asked, using a word I recognized as Mandarin for wife.

"*Tai tai,*" I replied.

He looked at our picture for a moment before saying, "Praising the Lord!"

I glanced at the photograph he had pointed out to me displayed on a shelf, taking the initiative this time with "Praising the Lord!"

"Praising the Lord!" he shared.

So for at least twenty minutes, perhaps longer, I repeated those three words so many times and something happened. The words became energized, warm, genuine, and precious.

Tears came to the eyes of both of us as we tasted the nectar of pure brotherhood. We looked at each other and repeated in unison, "Praising the Lord! Praising the Lord! Praising the Lord!" These words were the language of worship. The Holy Spirit knew and understood our thoughts.

Eventually the first pastor arrived, the remainder immediately following. In high excitement, the host explained what had been happening. Soon we were all joined in concert.

It was magnificent! As though we stood at the very portals of heaven, we all shared together those blessed words, "Praising the Lord!"

> *Let everything that hath breath praise the Lord.*
> *Praise the Lord.*
>
> Psalms 150:6

NINE

Discovering Heavenly Places

I was homeward bound!

The days had stretched into weeks and my eagerness to see my family intensified on each leg of the trip home. I had experienced so many things on this trip. I had come face-to-face with my pride. I was ashamed. Forgiveness was sought and obtained. I had witnessed a degree of self-sacrifice that I had not known before. I was embarrassed by my own self-centeredness and vowed to change. There were other positives as well.

Thousands had responded to the invitation to accept Jesus Christ as their Savior. Mrs. A would be reassured that I had not exaggerated the results of the crusades when I would give her a better accounting of the number who had responded to the invitations. I had been able to make many valuable contacts for future ministry. But perhaps the most important of all that happened was the growing knowledge and appreciation of God the Holy Spirit I had gained.

I exited China through Hong Kong, flying to the Philippines for a one hour stopover in Manila. While there I had a strange experience at the terminal. Over the public address system came a voice so familiar at first hearing, I supposed it to be someone of my acquaintance.

But then I caught the identity.

Walter A. Meier, radio spokesman for The Lutheran Hour, was

proclaiming the Gospel with clarity and unction via radio throughout the airport.

"'*For God so loved the world that He gave His only begotten son, that whosoever believeth in Him should not perish but have everlasting life.*' That quotation from the Bible," Meier continued, "contains the answer for a sick and dying world."

Back on board the plane, I stretched out in my comfortable accommodations sending my mind wandering back across my weeks in China and my captivating experiences. Clear to my memory came the words of Bob Pierce, "Millions across the world are dying for nothing. Oh, God, let me die for something!"

I thought of my vanity, my pride. I had faced China with the comforting thought that after a few weeks I would be returning to the good life again.

I thought of Mr. Lee, the Tientsin tycoon. After comparing his discipleship with my own, I realized mine wouldn't hold a candle to his. Oh, yes, I wanted to be a disciple of the Lord Jesus. I wanted to reach people with my writing. But there would be money involved.

Book royalties.

Payment per word for short stories, articles.

I settled back. Relaxing. Snoozing.

Awaking with a start, I realized we had touched down on Wake Island, an atoll in the Pacific.

I deplaned there for a short time to stretch my weary limbs.

When we were airborne again, I tried to resume my introspective thought. But my human demands overtook my spiritual inclinations and I slept all the way to Midway Island.

"There will be a two hour layover here," the stewardess announced. "I leave you here, but I will linger a few moments if any of you would like to experience the albatross."

"The albatross is known as the gooney bird, isn't it?" one of the other passengers asked.

"As we shall see!"

Looking out from my window seat onto that speck of sand in a vast world of water, the lines from the *Rime of the Ancient Mariner* came to my mind. I was unaware I was quoting them audibly until one of the other passengers joined me in unison.

> *"Day after day, day after day,*
> *we struck nor breath nor motion*
> *As idle as a painted ship upon a painted ocean.*
> *Water water everywhere, yet all the boards did shrink.*
> *Water water everywhere, but not a drop to drink."*

As if on a performing schedule, the moon slid into full brightness from behind a silvery cloud.

"Shhh!" the stewardess cautioned. "Everyone quiet now so we don't disturb the birds."

"Quiet, everybody!" she repeated.

The stewardess reached down and touched a talkative woman's arm to restrain her speach.

Fully a dozen awkwardly cumbersome giant birds had assembled at the top of a small dune beside the runway. One of the birds stepped out by himself, surveyed the situation, then began running down the hillside, like an airplane gaining speed for takeoff, finally going fast enough he spread his wings and flew off into the night.

The second bird appeared, repeating the action.

So it was, bird after bird, till all of them were flying.

"What if there weren't any hillsides?" asked the tourist.

"That's frequently the case," explained the stewardess. "When they face that situation, they wait for a strong wind to blow."

The two hours passed quickly and soon we were ready for

flight. Following takeoff and setting course toward Hawaii, I opened my Bible at random to Exodus. I turned a few pages then, coming to the twenty-fourth chapter, I noted verse seven: *All that God has said we will do, we will be obedient.*

I made a mental note of that commitment and continued leafing through the pages. I came to one of my favorite books in the Bible, Joshua. In verse eight of the first chapter, the Lord gave Joshua some specific and strategic information.

> *This book of the law shall not depart from your mouth, but you shall meditate in it day and night, that you may observe to do all that is written in it. Then you will make your way prosperous, and then you will have good success.*

The impact of that statement lies in three words.

OBSERVE TO DO

My heart was stirred. It was as if I were reading those words for the very first time, and it gave an amazing charge to my spirit.

In those three words, I found the key to living a genuinely Spirit- filled life. First, *observe.*

It was not a frivolous "take a look around" or "be sure you don't miss anything."

It was the directive to stay in the Word! As I study the Word I will learn how to experience a Spirit-filled life. His Word will be a lamp for my feet and the light for my path. The lamp will illuminate where I am this very moment. The light will shine ahead on my path to clearly reveal the way to get to my place of service.

It means I am to learn the truth of God's commands and promises provided in the Word. If I observe His promises, He will show me His will for my life. This requires more than the mouthing of words from a printed page. I must go beyond just reading Scriptures to a point of hiding them in my heart.

From this same passage in Joshua I learned the second step required to have a Spirit-filled life. This goes beyond the mental challenge of observing. It demands action.

To do! To do is to act, to take the teaching of Scripture and make it functional in your own life. That is the revelation for which I had been longing.

"Oh, God," I cried out above the drone of the engine to the bite of the propellers, "teach me concerning your word and show me how to obey the Scriptures that come from the Holy Spirit! Let it be a time of healing. Let my sins of pride and vanity be sublimated into love for the Lord Jesus."

It was happening with the aid of the Holy Spirit!

During those moments I was physically above the clouds, but my soul was far beyond in the heavenly bodies. I was dwelling in celestial places.

China had been the catalyst, but the Holy Spirit was and is my Guide!

I would never be able, nor would I try, to erase China's impact from my very soul!

. . .*those who hope in the Lord will renew their strength,*
they will soar on wings like eagles,
they will run and not grow weary,.
They will walk and not faint.
Isaiah 40:31

TEN

Charismatic
Renaissance

At the very beginning of the twentieth century, first a revival in Topeka, Kansas and then one on Azusa Street in Los Angeles brought a renewed interest in spiritual happenings unrecorded since the first century. Participants in these revivals experienced unusual manifestations and were labeled pentecostals and then later charismatics. It was not too long before church members divided into three groups because of these manifestations; charismatics, non-charismatics, and *anti*-charismatics.

Four things were commonly associated with this new movement: glossolalia (speaking in tongues), interpretation of tongues, prophecy, and physical healing. The first two and to some extent the third of the manifestations listed became divisive. But the fourth, healing, was a tenet of most Christian denominations, and my own circle of friends commonly prayed for healing, though perhaps most expected it to happen through the use of medical science.

Though neither my wife nor I are charismatics, our family has experienced divine intervention in the healing process.

Prior to the Jonas Salk development of a polio vaccine, we were living in Muskegon, Michigan, when a polio epidemic struck our community. In a period of only a few weeks, one hundred and twenty-six people, mainly children, were stricken. One of them was our neighbor girl. Three of our children, our oldest daughter, Naoma, and two of our sons, Lane and Max were afflicted.

Our children were immediately hospitalized and began receiving Sister Kenny treatments. We had never faced such a challenge before and we were confused in our understanding of how to pray. We decided not to pray for the healing of our children but rather to ask God for his will to be done. This gave us much peace.

At the time, Billy Graham was having his first city-wide crusade in Los Angeles during which several West Coast personalities were converted. This caught the attention of newspaper magnate William Randolph Hearst who dispatched a message to his network of papers across the country. It simply stated, "Puff Graham." Overnight, Billy Graham became one of those names that make news in our country.

When Billy heard of our family's tussle with polio, he had his massive crowd of thousands stand in silent prayer for our kids. We waited. Anita Galdean, neighbor and playmate, died as did one in ten during this large epidemic.

Meanwhile, the specialist looking after our children stood by Max's bed and putting his arm across Mrs. A's shoulder said, "Mommy, it looks like Max will lose the use of his right leg. We are arranging for a wheelchair plus many of the things you are sure to need."

We only prayed for God's will to be done. This gave us much peace.

The day came when the doctor said to Max's mother, "I'm not much on religion, but only a miracle explains what has happened to your son."

"A miracle in response to hundreds of prayers, Doctor."

Max, like his brother and sister, recovered to good health, as they are to this day.

Several years later, we were living in Warsaw, Indiana, and we wondered why we hadn't heard from Ken, Jr. all evening. He usually gave special word about what he was doing and where he was going, so we thought he was involved in something at the high school. We drove out there and saw nothing happening there at all. As we were checking out the high school, we heard an ambulance. Mrs. A said, "That could be Kenny," and we didn't pay any more attention at the time.

We went to the studio, and Melody, our daughter, was phoning us that the hospital had called with news of a car accident. We went to the hospital and met with the doctors who said they could do nothing for Kenny. He was in a coma. Later he was transferred to Fort Wayne where he could get special care. We rode over with him in the ambulance. That's when I grabbed his arm, and we prayed for him.

After the doctor had examined Kenny and came to talk with us he said, "Well, there is swelling in his head, so we can't x-ray to find out how serious this is. It looks very serious. He may be unconscious for a day, for a week, or for a year. We have no way of knowing at this time when he will regain consciousness. He may die before morning. He may die two days from now or a week from now. He may recover. All I can tell you now is your son is critically injured."

We went through the night waiting. We could go into his room in intensive care for just two minutes every hour. Each time we went in we grabbed his hand and prayed. Throughout the night Mrs. A whispered in his ear over and over again, "Anita is not dead. Anita is alive. Anita is alive!" She was afraid he was giving up, thinking he had killed his girl friend in the accident. Finally, getting on toward morning, we asked him if he could possibly hear us to squeeze our hands, and he did. What a moment! He continued progressing and was home within a week because he was doing so well.

In both instances, we knew it was through the supernatural power of God that the healing had been accomplished. We never thought of healing as a charismatic manifestation. But we knew that God had answered prayer through the power of the Holy Spirit.

There were many other times in my life when I was equally aware that the Holy Spirit was at work. Sometimes I was the observer; other times he was working on me.

When I first met Bob Walker, he headed the InterVarsity magazine *HIS*. Chicago-land abounded with editors and publishers determined to put a more professional touch to their numerous publications, amounting to secular savvy with here and now emphasis on practical faith.

Freshly graduated from Northwestern's Medill School of Journalism, Bob Walker gave that exact slant to the InterVarsity publication. *HIS* became a how-to-do-it trail blazer for many quality hungry publishers. Victor Cory, with his newly founded Scripture Press Organization, led the pack. Primarily, he had a publication known as *Church School Promoter* which abounded in grapevines on how to grow a successful Sunday school, but unfortunately lacked the professional touch of the InterVarsity trail blazer.

As quickly as possible, Mr. Cory arranged to meet Mr. Walker. In that one meeting, a spark of inevitable rapport quickly ignited into the full flame of purpose and identification.

To his delight, Victor Cory learned that Bob Walker had developed a staff at InterVarsity who could ably take over *HIS* magazine and maintain its momentum of success. Also, Bob Walker was looking for an avenue through which he could share his idea for Christian journalism with evangelicals geared to improve both the writing and layout expertise of their publications.

Victor Cory hired Bob Walker, and forces were put in motion that would change the image of Christian journalism forever. Immediately, *Church School Promoter* began looking more like *Saturday Evening Post* than a Sunday School publication.

Church School Promoter became *Sunday School Promoter*

for a couple of issues that is. Then the name of the magazine was *Sunday Magazine* with "School Promoter" sublimated. Soon everything was gone except *Sunday Magazine*, and the evangelical world had a magazine every bit as perceived and expedited as the best of the secular magazines. It was great sport for those of us in the evening journalism classes on the Wheaton campus to watch the magazine and then compare what we saw there with our own development as writers.

Bob Walker bought several things from me, usually short stories. He grew his own writers! That is, he would find someone with aptitude, and then invest hours of time showing them how to write like pros.

I was fortunate to become one of the candidates with whom he spent quality time.

Not content to simply upgrade his *Church School Promoter* publication, he added the Walker touch to Sunday School lessons and established some take-home papers. This provided continuity of writing opportunities for me.

I need to profile Bob Walker so you will understand his impact upon young people, primarily those in the journalism classes at Wheaton. The first look at Bob Walker gave one the impression of an Ivy League don. He had a secular air about him, and he would proceed through an entire lecture without the use of any "party lines" by which many evangelicals identified themselves.

He had a special interest in New England where he found Episcopal Churches with Bible-saturated worship formats but lacking in spiritual life. He carefully examined the intellectual bias of such Ivy League schools as Harvard, Princeton, and Yale discovering that, in their fledgling years as institutions of higher learning, these Ivy League schools were not unlike the Moody Bible Institute of his time.

In his New England explorations, he came upon a man by the name of Howard Bredesen, a Reformed Church clergyman, who was preaching and teaching the pentecostal message in his church. Not content to experience charismatic dimensions in his own congregation, he began reaching out to others. He found a host of congregations where they hungered for the teaching of the Scriptures, particularly as it related to the pentecostal message.

Bob Walker heard what was happening and arranged to meet Howard Bredesen. What Bob's initial reaction may have been to the charismatic message is not public information, but it was soon obvious that the "secularized" Bob Walker became a charismatic proponent.

On one occasion, at the *Christian Life* office while discussing an article I was doing for the magazine, Bob and I sat alone in his office and he gave me a warm evaluation of what he considered to be happening to the charismatic influence on evangelicalism in that day. Strangely, he reported his information to me in the third person, not as though it was something private, and yet I saw it as being very personal.

Bob Walker became a new person.

It was beautiful to see!

He was excited about what he saw in the church. As cold orthodoxy became vibrant pentecostalism, Bob committed his Christian life to the charismatic movement.

The American evangelical churches began dividing themselves into two camps, the charismatic and the non-charismatic.

In many instances, non-charismatic became *anti*-charismatic.

The devil had a heyday!

Christian Life magazine subscriptions plummeted and eventually it merged with the new *Charisma* magazine.

For a period of time, evangelism waned and the crusade was geared toward winning "converts" from the non-charismatic persuasion to the charismatic.

In my own case, I got on someone's mailing list and received a persistence of propaganda geared toward persuading me to become an all out pentecostal. The image of the *Holy Rollers* of my childhood came to mind. While I did not become *anti*-charismatic, I did become quite obsessed with the conviction that there was nothing to be had in any other relationship with the Holy Spirit that I was not already enjoying.

"Lord," I remember praying, "if there is anything relating to the work of the Holy Spirit which I need in my life, please let me have it. Remove any resistance I may have toward these pentecostal ideas prevalent today."

The Gospel Films Ministry, which began in our woodland bungalow near Muskegon, Michigan, experienced the influence of the charismatic ministry. As the result of the prayer I had prayed asking God to give me anything I might be missing in the ministry of the Holy Spirit, I began toying with an idea for a film which we subsequently called *Centerville Awakening*.

In *Centerville Awakening* we endeavored to show the ministry of the Holy Spirit in changing and encouraging the lives of Christians without involving manifestations of the Holy Spirit. In fact, these were not even mentioned in our script.

Until then, our Gospel Films board involved a handful of members who were silent *anti*-charismatics, who now emerged in full articulation voicing their views.

Bob Walker gave us helpful publicity in what remained of the once booming audience of *Christian Life* magazine. He ran the *Centerville Awakening* story, plus put my picture on the cover of the magazine. This was prior to the advent of e-mail, and we were inundated with pro and con reactions. Because of the spiritual zeal of the pentecostals, the phenomenon mentioned previously was suddenly perceived as a literal crusade, not to win souls to a knowledge of Jesus Christ as their Savior but to win non-charismatics to the charismatic camp.

Of course this perception was not always based solely upon simple pentecostal exhuberance, but frequently on the fact that some pentecostals did feel it was their calling to ensure that all Christians experience the same manifestations of the Holy Spirit as themselves.

I remember receiving an unsigned letter from one antagonist:

> *Dear Brother Ken,*
> *We have a large body of brothers and sisters, all of whom have experienced the wonderful gift of tongues who are praying for you that one day you, too, will experience "this wonderful deepening of your spiritual life."*

He then enclosed a mimeographed sheet that described a procedure to help people pray themselves into speaking in tongues This sheet contained suggestions of the combination of letters of the alphabet which, if repeated in monotone, would eventually loosen the tongue so that one could experience the joy of glossolalia.

I was also guaranteed that if I would completely relax and do the alphabet combination over and over for as long as it took, I would be assured that my tongue would be loosened, and I would speak with the language of the angels!

One day I went into the woods behind our house carrying my red colored *Youth for Christ* Bible. I prayed, "Lord, I almost feel estranged from this Book. Please help me. I don't want this to be a Charismatic Bible or a Non-Charismatic Bible, a Calvinist Bible or an Armenian Bible, Baptist or Lutheran, Presbyterian or whatever."

Weeping like a child, if ever I could have experienced glossolalia it should have been at that moment. I cried out, "Oh Lord, if you've ever heard a prayer, hear this one." Then, deliberate emphasis on every word, I cried out into the trees with my gaze heavenward, "Oh, Lord, please make this my Bible! Make it Ken Anderson's Bible."

God answered that prayer!

In that exact moment!

At first I almost felt as though I had had my tongue loosened to pray in strange utterances.

"Please, Lord," I whispered, "if there is anything I am missing in my life, if there is anything I need to serve You better, I won't resist it Lord . . . whatever it may be."

I waited.

A vast peace came into my being.

It was wonderful!

Meanwhile, however, unrest fomented among members of the Gospel Films board, skimmed primarily from the publicity in *Christian Life* magazine. Tension came to a head the night we showed the final edited interlock of the film to our board at the studio. It felt at times as if the very demons of hell permeated the entire studio area. As the film was shown, however, a quiet peace came over the small group of men assembled to have a look.

As the film concluded, one of the less ardent of the *anti's*, an especially good friend of mine, said to the chairman, "Boy, Jack, to me that story didn't seem like the pentecostals. That's exactly what I believe about the Holy Spirit."

Open discussion tossed the matter pro and con. Finally, one of the more outspoken members of the opposition made a motion that we not release the film. Thus came the evening's most heated discussion. Finally, I spoke up suggesting we have a showing to pastors in the community who are known to be non-charismatic, and they would influence those pastors of churches represented by board members who were strongly anti-charismatic.

We organized our first pastors' interlock viewing in Grand Rapids, so the opposition members left. Included in attendance was the pastor of the most outspoken members of the board, a man who had given his people extensive teaching on such topics as "Modern

Pentecostalism, is it of the Lord or of the Devil?"

At the close of the pastors' showing in Grand Rapids, the pastors sat silent for several moments. Their reactions were positive and heart moving.

The non-charismatic pastor of the church attended by most of board in opposition to the film even recommended it. He had the courage to admit it presented a Biblical view on the indwelling presence of the Holy Spirit in the life of a Christian.

I was not alone! There was a beautiful sense of an abiding presence. The Holy Spirit was at work just as Jesus had promised He would be.

I will ask the Father and He will give you another
Helper, that He may be with you forever.
John 14:16

ELEVEN

The
Spirit-filled
Life

The following day, alone in the woods near our home in Michigan, I grasped my Bible and, holding it between me and the sky, thanked God for making it my personal message from Him. Then I began to change. An engaging new frame of reference entered my mind . . . *Layology.*

That word has energized my thought process as it relates to the Scriptures more than any other stimuli I have encountered.

Layology, admittedly often whimsical, is that observation and study of the Scriptures advantageous to those believers who, although lowly in status, have limitless potential for value in the service of the work of the Kingdom. It may be defined as the layman's role in ministry.

In the initial three verses of the third chapter of First Corinthians, the Apostle Paul writes:

> *Brothers, I could not address you as spiritual but as worldly . . . mere infants in Christ. I gave you milk, not solid food, for you were not ready for it. Indeed, you are still not ready.*
> *You are still worldly. For since there is jealousy and quarreling among you, are you not worldly? Are you not acting like mere men?*

In *Layology*, one is not so much involved with interpretation of the Scripture as in a practical application of it. So, in the case of these three verses of 1 Corinthians 3, my process has been to reverse the teaching mode here.

Paul appears to be speaking of milk as simple things in the Scriptures, easy for anyone to understand. Milk was not solid food that dealt with those concepts which challenge the deepest thinking of intellectuals.

However, I began to see "milk" as those aspects of the Bible which greatly challenge the intellect. The solid food is that in Scripture which takes us to a deep and significant discipleship. It is that which causes Ken Anderson to be a better Christian today than he was yesterday . . . more tender hearted . . . more of a humble servant!

By approaching charismatic theology as profound content, over which believers debate to great lengths, it has often created further divisions rather than developing more candidates for God's sheer blessing and guidance . . . apart from any spectacular manifestations.

Try, for example, 2 Timothy 3:16:

> *All Scripture is God-breathed and is useful for teaching, rebuking, correcting and training in righteousness, so that the man of God may be thoroughly equipped for every good work.*

This passage indicates the purpose of the Scriptures.

Is there anything there that prescribes how or what God will use to equip us for every good work?

No!

Did you see anything about any of the gifts of the Holy Spirit?

No!

No ONE gift is singled out as necessary in order to be equipped for every good work!

So, you see, you and I have only to search the Scriptures to find what God's will is for our lives, what work He has for us to do, how we can best serve Him, and live at peace with all our brother and sister Christians.

Pure *Layology* holds the key to understand some of the simplest statements God has made to his children through the ages. How many desperate believers find themselves in a quandary as to God's will for their lives, have found respite in the words of Jeremiah 29:11:

I know the plans that I have for you, declares the Lord, plans to prosper you and not to harm you, plans to give you hope and a future.

And note the claim from the *Layologian* manual – to those who consult Proverbs 3:5-6:

Trust in the Lord with all your heart, and lean not on your own understanding; in all your ways acknowledge Him, and He will make your paths straight.

That, you will particularly note, is a part out of God's contract with his people. Sheer *Layology*!

Your part – *Trust in the Lord with all your heart, and lean not unto your own understanding, in all your ways acknowledge Him.*

God's part – . . . *and He shall direct your paths.*

Pardon the "commercial," but let me tell you about my book, *Bible Based Prayer Power,* Copyright 2000, Thomas Nelson Publishers, Nashville, Tennessee.

In writing this book, I needed a key scripture as the basis for the thesis for the approach. A friend of mine suggested John 15:7, where Jesus said, "*If you remain in me, and my words remain in you, ask whatever you wish and it will be given you.*" In numerous places in the Bible we are told that God will answer our prayers, often speaking of the "desires" of our hearts.

In all honesty, I couldn't put the element of such promises together.

Then one day, we were in Honduras working on the film *Flight Plans* for Missionary Aviation Fellowship. Don Robertson, veteran MAF pilot, was helping me find several locations for film scenes and took me out across the rugged terrain of the hinterlands of Central America.

We began fellowshipping. The air control office in Tegucigalpa had no other planes but his which had registered flight plans for that area.

"I always carry my Bible with me," Don said, finding his log book and retrieving the Bible he always carried with it.

"I have lots of down time," he stated, "and it's good to have the Word with you to bone up on your expertise, or lack thereof, in the Scriptures."

I saw that he thumbed his way into the Psalms though I could not see exactly where.

"Why do people complain when their prayers are not answered?" I asked

He hesitated a moment as he had me at his full command.

"What bothers me," I continued, "are the many strong indications God gives us that we are able to get our prayers answered. But it doesn't seem to always hold true. Take, for example, one of my favorite verses, John 15: 7. *If you remain in me and my words remain in you, ask whatever you wish and it will be given you.*"

Don then quoted Psalm 37:4, "*Delight yourself in the Lord, and He will give you the desires of your heart."*

"What's the difference between this verse and John 15:7?" I asked in frustration.

I saw the etch of pain come upon his face. I realized why. My missionary pilot friend wasn't a candidate for Bible language arguments.

"How do you interpret the word *desires?*" he asked.

"I take it just the way it is written," I replied.

"So did I for a long time. Then one day flying alone I had a great need for an answered prayer. I read this verse, and the Holy Spirit revealed something to me."

Don looked intently at his Bible for a moment and continued, "If you delight yourself in the Lord, then the desires of *your heart* are interrelated with Him. I no longer have my desires, but the Lord's desires! The Scriptures were showing me that if I want my prayers answered, His desires must be my desires."

Once more the Holy Spirit, the Comforter who Jesus had promised would come, was calling me . . . yes, guiding me . . . into the way to obtain and maintain a spirit-filled life. My desires must be aligned with God's desires. My soul cried out for that exact kind of relationship with Him. I had read Jeremiah's passage many times before, but it now would impact me for the rest of my life.

"I know the plans I have for you," declares the Lord,
"plans to prosper you and not to harm you,
plans to give you hope and a future.
Then you will call upon me and come and pray to me,
and I will listen to you.
You will seek me and find me
when you seek me with all your heart.
Jeremiah 29:11-13

TWELVE

The Stockholm Experience

We were completing our extensive tour as we searched for the most receptive places for our film ministry. The tour had taken us throughout the Orient and now we were in the Middle East still laying the groundwork for Christian ministry, which eventually became the heart beat of the film *Something to Die For*.

"*Subhana Allah, Humma Wa Bihundicka. . .*"

This, the second morning prayer call in the predawn darkness, sent me stumbling to my feet, groggy, angry and disgusted at such rude incivility. I was in a complaining mood.

Although I had learned that when missionary organizations developed a place of ministry, it seemed Muslims invariably erected a mosque and prayer tower adjacent. I sat at the breakfast table in the nurses' residence of the American Mission Hospital in Basra, Iraq and complained. I was irritated.

"How can you endure such noise?" I asked.

"It is not noise to me," replied a nurse from Michigan. "Whenever I hear the Muslim call to prayer, I take it as a call to me as well, and I stop and spend several minutes praying for my many Muslim friends."

That was one of the greatest rebukes I had ever received, and one that I can never forget!

Proceeding on westward in the following weeks, I made valuable contacts in Beirut, Jerusalem, Cairo, Athens, Rome, Geneva, Paris, Amsterdam, Brussels, Berlin, and Copenhagen.

Then, bone weary, but nonetheless exuberant over the many friends I had made as we opened doors of opportunity, I headed northward to Oslo, then Stockholm.

Excitement touched my body as I landed at the Stockholm airport. I'm pedigree Swedish, you see, thrilled with the prospect of winning Swedish teenagers to the Lord through films we had produced.

My pulse was quite active as the plane settled down in Stockholm. At the airport to greet me was Haakan Cronsoe, the editor of the Swedish edition of *Guideposts,* as well as our key contact throughout Scandanavia.

Adding a touch of levity to our fellowship, he said, "You know, brother Ken, we speak English with a Swedish *accident!*" Almost in the same breath he added, "Just put your billfold in your suitcase and keep it locked." We didn't even check in at the hotel desk for he had used his American Express card. He forbid me to use mine. He announced that we had a luncheon scheduled for tomorrow with thirty pastors and that all the expenses were already paid.

We conversed together in my room for a time of fellowship, and then he was gone.

I sat for several moments basking in recollections of all that God had allowed me to experience. I thought of my pastor friend in China and his single English phrase, "Praising the Lord."

Lost in my reflections, I thought I heard music, and yet . . . it was as though I had been at a concert and enjoyed a great symphony . . . newly composed, artistically rendered. The music ceased and it seemed that I was walking from the concert hall even as the music permeated my being.

Praise began flowing from my mouth. I was not aware of

forming words as they flowed from my innermost being. There was no music . . . no symphony . . . yet the otherworldly feeling continued. No music, just the feeling.

And thus it was with me as I lay sprawled on the bed.

"Praising the Lord!" was the outcry.

"Thank you Lord," quickly followed.

"Paising the Lord!" I cried out again.

I tried to be quiet. But there was no silence . . . only continuing praise.

"Praising the Lord! Praising the Lord! Thank You! Thank You!" On and on, although I can't recall how long . . . maybe half an hour . . . perhaps an entire hour, the praises continued. My praises were not spoken in some unknown tongue. My heavenly language . . . the language of my soul . . . was expressed in English, my native tongue.

I don't know how long it was before I arose and turned on the light by my bed. But, exhausted, I responded to the call of sleep. Like the wonderful sensation of satisfaction that follows a concert, I lay back down and relaxed into a peaceful sleep.

Awakening sometime later, I was intensely aware of an overwhelming sense of cleansing. I was clean. My whole body felt clean. Could this be the baptism charismatics speak of? If so, there was no speaking in tongues, no words of prophesy, no physical healing, but I knew God had filled me with His presence and I felt clean.

I reached for my Bible longing to understand what was happening to me. Turning to I Corinthians, I soon realized what it was.

I had traveled half-way around the world continually seeking the spirit-filled life. There in that hotel room in Stockholm, Sweden, I had a new appreciation of I Corinthians 13:12.

Now we see but a poor reflection as in a mirror;
then we shall see face-to-face; now I know in part;

then I shall I know fully even as I am fully known.

After my total submission to God, I was experiencing the fullness of God's presence! I was beginning to know the joy of the Spirit-filled life. I truly had found something . . . no . . . Someone . . . to die for. His fullness continues to remain with me.

My search was not in vain. The changeless Holy Spirit filled me and continually fills me with His presence. He did exactly what Christ had said He would do.

When He, the Spirit of truth is come,
He will guide you into all truth!
John 16:13

Epilogue

Wanting More

The start of the Spirit-filled life begins here, *"If we confess our sins, he is faithful and just and will forgive us our sins and purify us from all unrighteousness."* 1 John 1:9 with these results: *"If anyone is in Christ, he is a new creation; the old has gone, the new has come!"* 2 Corinthians 5:17.

This book is a record of my personal relationship with God that may be accurately described as *wanting more*. Those two words, however, may be frightening for some. When you are experiencing a peace and joy that is indescribable and previously unknown, the idea of wanting more could be both overwhelming and seemingly impossible.

Wanting *some* of a Spirit-filled life may even be frightening if your experiences with people claiming to have such a relationship have been negative. Causing legitimate fear and uncertainty is the well-publicized behavior identified with cults and religious extremists. Much of current society is willing to be considered spiritual or religious, but few seem eager to be known as Spirit-filled.

Consequently, suggesting that you should be seeking a Spirit-filled life may raise some legitimate concerns. It may be expedient for me to consider that possibility.

In spite of any misgivings you may have, every true Christian reaches a time when *knowing* God better is more important than knowing more *about* Him. The One who provides such freedom as you are experiencing through His grace can be trusted and sought after! The knowledge that your sins are truly forgiven is for the mind what peace is to the spirit.

Along with the satisfaction in your Christian life, you may continually face questions never considered before. What does it really mean to be a Christian? How am I different? What do people think of me as a Christian? What does God have for me? What does it mean to "serve" God?

When did you find answers to those questions? Did it happen that first day or during the first month after you accepted Christ? Of course not! However, if after several months or years you are still asking the same questions, there should be some concern?

The idiom, *wanting more*, may be less troublesome if I share an analogy regarding friendship. Meeting an individual and making an acquaintance can be a momentary thing, but building a friendship . . . developing a relationship . . . occurs over time. One or both individuals are *wanting more* knowledge about each other. There are questions to be answered and information to be exchanged if a casual meeting is to become a friendship. This process results in changes which enhance the growing relationship. We are willing to make changes because we want to know the other person more . . . to please them. That's the way it works with God, too. The changes that will come in your life because you are getting to know God more will happen because *you* want to change. God does not force you to change.

The willingness to change is in direct proportion to the degree of trust in and love for the other person. Through the years I have learned I can trust God, and He is the only one I can totally trust. No one loves me like He does. That does not mean, however, that we will have roses without thorns or sunny skies without rain. There are no mountains unless there are valleys, and it is important to have both night and day.

You, like most of the rest of us, have seen individuals you absolutely don't want to be like. This can create a problem if they claim to be a Christian. It is doubly troublesome if they claim to be living a Spirit-filled life and expect you to be like them. When you feel that happening, it is time to be cautious.

It is important to remember there can only be a counterfeit when there is a real thing to imitate. God is not looking for counterfeit or copy cat Christians. He doesn't intend for you to be like anyone else. Are you afraid to be unique? Are you afraid to be different from what you are or always have been? Do you trust God to make you better or more like Him?

Another reason people become fearful about a Spirit-filled life is because they know so little about who the Holy Spirit is and what He is supposed to do for and with us. We have been taught so little about the Holy Spirit. The unknown with its uncertainty is reason to be afraid *unless* you completely trust the one leading you into the unknown. Perfect love . . . perfect trust . . . casts out fear, but we do not have perfect love or perfect trust, and so we continue to be afraid until the love and trust increases.

Are you afraid God will ask you to do something unreasonable or foolish? Are you afraid He will ask you to go some place where you will be miserable? Do friends do that? No! God, who has called us friends, will certainly not treat us with disdain. After all, He gave His life for us.

No one knows you better than God does. He knows precisely what you need in order to become the best possible you. You *can* trust Him. He does not operate on the trial and error method, and God the Holy Spirit will guide you into only the very best.

Throughout this book I have shared my heart-cry to know God better, to experience all He has for me. There was a moment in

Stockholm when I entered into the fullness of His Spirit. I remain in that relationship as long as I continue to totally surrender to Him as I did at that moment in Stockholm.

For me, it was years of struggle and searching, but that was not God's fault. It was not that He was unwilling to provide the fullness of His Spirit for me at an earlier time. The delay was caused by my unwillingness to accept the Holy Spirit and His leadership in my life, to totally align my desires with His desires. As long as I wanted to be the decision maker, the Spirit-filled life was impossible to attain.

Anyone searching to know God better will come face-to-face with these challenging questions. What is a Spirit-filled life? Do I want to accept all God has for me? What must I do to obtain a Spirit-filled life?

I encourage you to depend on Luke 11:13 which states,

"If you then, though you are evil, know how to give good gifts to your children, how much more will your Father in heaven give the Holy Spirit to those who ask him?"

Do you want this gift the Father has ready to give you?

Earlier, I referred to three words that provided for me a key to living a genuinely Spirit-filled life. They are found in verse eight of the first chapter of Joshua.

"This book of the law shall not depart from your mouth, but you shall meditate in it day and night that you may observe to do all that is written in it. Then you will make your way prosperous, and then you will have good success."

The three words are OBSERVE TO DO. In the following pages you will find a practical application of that directive presented as a study guide in your search for a Spirit-filled life. Approach it as a personal exercise or invite others to join with you in this journey to know God better, to find and accept all that He has planned especially for you.

Appendix

For Personal
or
Group Study

by Dr. Marvin G. Baker

Our Guidebook, the Holy Bible

The hope of every Christian lies in the truths presented in the Bible. Arguments about the teachings of the Bible have torn families, congregations, and denominations apart, but the Bible continues to withstand all onslaughts. That is no surprise for Psalm 119:89 declares, *"Your word, O Lord, is eternal; it stands firm in the heavens."*

That truth alone would be reason for using the Bible as our guidebook, but let me add two additional reasons. The Bible is inspired. *"All Scripture is God-breathed . . ."* 2 Timothy 3:16. The Holy Spirit, the focus of this study, was the power source. *". . . men spoke from God as they were carried along by the Holy Spirit."* 2 Peter 1:21.

By the investigations of Bible truths found in the Scriptures, and the application of these truths to the faith we confidently live by as revealed in Romans 10:17, Christians can enjoy an abundant life whether or not they have experienced charismatic manifestations.

The Trinity and You

The Holy Spirit, the power source for the Bible, is the Trinity's representative on earth today. He is the one who is available to every believer around the world simultaneously. Did you catch the implications? Jesus Christ, God's *only* Son, has already asked the Father to give *you* the Holy Spirit. That's right! When you are able to truly comprehend that the Triune God – the creator of heaven and earth – wants to dwell within you and to be in constant fellowship with you, it is overwhelming. Read Psalm 8:3-5 to grasp the significance of how much God really wants you.

Consider the words in 1 Corinthians 6:19-20.

> *"Do you not know that your body is a temple of the Holy Spirit, who is in you, whom you have received from God? You are not your own; you were bought at a price. Therefore honor God with your body."*

As you comprehend all of this, excitement is unavoidable. Realizing that anticipation is often the greatest joy, begin now to anticipate what God has planned for you! Prepare for your personal spiritual growth by looking for ways to see God at work.

Anticipate becoming a new person!

Throughout this study you are taking additional steps in your search to know God, the Holy Spirit, and seeking a life filled and directed by Him. If it is to be more than an intellectual exercise, it should begin with this commitment: *"I desire to do your will, O my God . . ."* Psalm 40:8, and Psalm 119: 16 *"I delight in your decrees; I will not neglect your word."* In the light of that commitment, consider these three things: purposes, helps, and lessons.

The PURPOSES

1. To learn more *about* the Holy Spirit
2   To strengthen your personal relationship with the Holy Spirit
3   To review another's steps toward a satisfying relationship with the Holy Spirit

4.   To gain proficiency in using the Bible in this process of knowing the Holy Spirit more

Purposes, if clearly stated, need no explanation. Although suggestions may be made, how they are to be achieved is a personal matter. Each must fight in his own armor, but every person in the group is engaged in the same battle.

The HELPS
   A. For the Leader
       1.   Creating an environment for learning
       2.   Strive for humility in leadership
       3.   Using group dynamics to enhance
       4.   Decisions to be made by the group
   B. For Others
       1.   Come anticipating growth opportunities
       2.   Participate to enhance growth for everyone

URGENT: Whenever individuals begin a sincere seeking after God and all that He has for them, they will undoubtedly be targeted by our enemy, Satan. There will be a battle!

Do not participate in this study with prejudice in your heart either in favor of or in opposition toward the manifestations of and by the Holy Spirit. Each person must be open to receive all that God has for them. In the event of dispute, the Group Leader shall ask for immediate silence. If that request is not forthcoming, the meeting will be adjourned until the next scheduled time and place.

For the Leader
   The success of discussion groups rests heavily on the leader. Experience dictates there should be attention to the four

areas listed above.

1. Creating an environment for learning.

These are things dictated by common sense but sometimes overlooked.

a. Ample space for each participant
b. Fresh air
c. Comfortable seating
d. A welcoming atmosphere
e. Adequate materials. In spite of the fact that each person is to provide his own, you will always need extras. Sharpened pencils, writing paper, books or magazines to serve as "writing desks"
f. Resource materials including various translations of the Bible, Bible concordance, and a copy of Ken Anderson's book, *Where to Find It In the Bible.*

2. Striving for humility

Dare to seek an atmosphere of unobtrusive humility as the basic trait of your leadership and your personality. Unobtrusive humility is impossible unless the Holy Spirit is in your life.

Have you ever noticed how false humility appears in the life of someone who is, for whatever reason, trying to display a humble attitude? I think you will find, that for the most part, humility for which we are concerned will be a byproduct of the entire study of this book.

Take at least an hour with the Scriptures below and encourage every member of the group to do the same. Seek to discover what each verse has to do with humility.

NOTE: Scriptures related to humility: Numbers 12:3, Psalms 84:10, Proverbs 18:12, 22:4, and 27:2, Isaiah 29:19, Jeremiah 9:23-24,

Zephaniah 2:3, 12, Matthew 20:26-28, Luke 9:58, 14:8-11, and 18:10-14, John 3:30, Romans 7:18-25, 12:3, and 12:16, 2 Corinthians 4:5-7. Ephesians 3:8, and 1 Peter 5:6

3. Using group dynamics to facilitate learning

Whether this study is scheduled for a Sunday School class or a Bible study group which meets at another time and location, some things apply in either situation. Here are things that are common to both:

a.   People want to know the names of others in the group.

b.   Interaction is expected. The leader is to facilitate not dominate. Members interact better if the seating is in a circular arrangement instead of rows.

c.   Courtesy is a necessity. That means no one can be allowed to monopolize the session. Every member is a learner! Every member is a teacher! Not everyone is verbal and comfortable sharing in a group setting, and will most likely be reluctant to interject their ideas. You, the leader, must see that each person has at least one chance per session to share with the group.

d.   As leader, you will be expected to know more about the content of each chapter than anyone else. Demonstrate your leadership skills by having some questions ready when an awkward lull comes. That does *not* imply there is never a time for silence!

4. Decisions to be made by the group

There will be a greater loyalty and commitment to the group if they are allowed to participate in setting the ground rules. Let them all participate in answering these questions:

a.   Are we committed to keep the meeting a "study session?"

b.   Do we agree the topic will stay focused on "Seeking a Spirit-filled life?"

c.   How often will we meet? And for how long?

d. Where will the meetings be held?

e. Will the same person lead each sesson?

f. How much time of each meeting will be set for the Bible study?

g. Will we have refreshments? If so, what will they be? Who fixes them? Who pays?

h. Will each person be responsible for bringing his own study materials? (*Confessions of a Non-charismatic, Seeking a Spirit-filled Life,* and a Bible)

i. Will visitors be encouraged to attend?

j. Other questions that may arise

NOTE: If any changes prove to be desirable, discuss alternatives and let any changes be a decision by the group and not a leader's presumption. Then honor your commitments!

For Participants

I can think of only a few times when working together is irrelevant or undesirable when applied to any Christian activity. As iron sharpens iron, so friends may sharpen friends especially in Bible study. There are two challenges:

1. Come anticipating growth opportunities

Little learning is done by osmosis in spite of the fact many have tried it. Learning is an active process. The results are usually in direct proportion to the effort expended.

a. Come with a spirit of expectancy, knowing that God, the Holy Spirit, will be meeting with you.

b. Come anticipating to learn how to be a better observer of what the Holy Spirit is doing.

2. Participate to enhance growth for everyone

I am a bit amused by those individuals who say, "I don't like to comment in class because I learn so much more by listening." That's nice that you do listen, but imagine if everyone in the classroom felt the same way. Silence is not always golden. A classroom of listeners only is a classroom of 'takers.' They are willing to take whatever they can get and whenever they can get it. Giving in a Bible study is a blessing.

   a. Come expecting to share what the Holy Spirit is doing in your life.

   b. Come to hear what the Holy Spirit is doing in the lives of others.

The SESSIONS

Topics	Lesson Titles	Chapter Titles
1 Touched	The Search Is Begun	Father Versus Son
2 Warned	Differences and Disappointments	The Quiet Way
3 Called	Chosen for Ministry	God's Messenger
4 Strengthened	When the Pressure Is On	On the Spot
5 Compelled	Amazing Opportunities	Many Facets of Learning
6 Convicted	The Price of Pride	Martyrs and My Pride Syndrome
7 Helped	Total Commitment	Facing Martyrdom
8 Blessed	Fruit of the Spirit	The Holy Spirit at Work
9 Directed	Finding Answers	Discovering Heavenly Places
10 Challenged	Spiritual Renewal	Charismatic Renaissance
11 Commissioned	Prepared for a Purpose	The Spirit-filled Life
12 Sustained	Maintaining a Spirit-filled Life	The Stockholm Experience

A time, a topic, a title, do not a lesson make, but they are important components of any learning opportunity. Every class I ever attended had its own agenda though at times I was uncertain if it had been planned prior to the time set for the class to begin.

Each person attending a Bible study, or almost any meeting, comes with some expectations though often neither clearly perceived nor articulated. The time will be better spent if you have an inkling of what is expected. Consequently, I suggest this agenda for each session. Three simple things: fellowship, faith, and facts with limited augmentation. Here is the agenda:

1. Fellowship

Always have a welcoming attitude and atmosphere. You are coming to learn not to be labeled. So be friendly while keeping in mind that the primary purpose of the meeting is for Bible study. Keep focused. You are consuming God's time as well as that of each member of the group.

2. Faith

Begin your study time with a prayer of praise and adoration. This could include a prayer chorus or words of a hymn focused on the Holy Spirit. The solemn melodic theme of *"Spirit of the Living God"* could be used at the opening and closing of your session.

NOTE: Other gospel choruses focusing on the Holy Spirit are: *"Holy Spirit, Thou Art Welcome In This Place," "Surely the Presence of the Lord Is In This Place,"* or hymns such as *"Spirit of God, Descend upon My Heart," "Holy Spirit, Light Divine,"* and *"Fill Me Now."*

3. Facts

There is a place for opinions, and I am positive they will be shared freely, but the primary concern is what the Bible has to say and how it relates to our pursuit of a Spirit-filled life.

   a.   Topic and chapter Title - On the surface, what relationship do you see between them?

   b.   Bible focus

   c.   Discovery and Discussion: application of verses to your life. Do you find any parallels from the book?

   e.   Pause with heads bowed after the final study question for a time of personal reflection and a deeper commitment to a Spirit-filled life.

   d.   Assignment for next week

4. Faith

Closing with prayer of thanksgiving and theme chorus

5. Fellowship

SESSION ONE: The Search Is Begun

Forewarn and Chapter 1 - Father versus Son

Fellowship:

Icebreaker: (A suggestion) At the start of the first few sessions try to learn one thing about each member in the group. This might accomplish two things: (1) keep the fellowship time brief and (2) help build relationships. So for this session please limit your introduction to just your name.

Faith:

Prayer of Adoration

Song of commitment: *Spirit of the Living God*

Facts:

Key Phrase: Touched by the Spirit

Introduction: Thousands of your fellow Christians can witness to the tremendous change in store for you if you are willing to live a Spirit-filled life. You may wonder why instruction about the person and work of the Holy Spirit has been neglected if it is so beneficial for a Christian. We are not charged with answering that, but the question remaining is what we will do about the Biblical directive *"be filled with the Spirit."* You can be assured that when you are seeking a Spirit-filled life, you are participating in one of the most exciting experiences you will ever know.

This is not intended to be an in-depth study of the person and work of the Holy Spirit. We'll leave that to the theologians. This is simply a study in the process of seeking the Holy Spirit whereby we can compare one laymen's experience with our own.

Bible Readings: Ephesians 5:18 and John 13:35

Discovery and Discussion: As you begin this Bible study, consider this story.

Four men often played golf together. Three were Christians and usually shared their spiritual journey as they played. The Holy Spirit began working in the life of the non-Christian. Finally, one day he brought a pocket New Testament to the golf course. Before they teed off, one of his friends asked about the bulge in his shirt pocket. All three were amazed when he pulled out the New Testament.

"I've listened almost every week to you guys talking about faith," he said. "I've known you long enough to realize you aren't lying to me. Can any of you take this New Testament and show me how to become a Christian? I'd just like to read it for myself."

The ability to quote a Bible verse without knowing where it is found is like having a friend without knowing where they live. How do you find them when you need them?

Confessions of a Non-charismatic is one man's account of seeking the Spirit-filled life. Each person's journey will be different, but Ken Anderson's experience may help us identify steps on our way. This Study Guide provides a Biblical basis for his search and for ours, too.

Study Questions:

1. Why do you think he used the word "Forewarn" instead of "Foreword?"

2. What is the basis for your faith in the Bible? (2 Timothy 3:16 and 2 Peter 1:21)

3. The Old Testament is the account of God, the Gospels record the work of the Son, but the work of the Holy Spirit is scattered throughout the Bible. The relationship between the Holy Spirit and individuals becomes very clear in the Book of Acts. Why do think God chose that time in history to show us that relationship?

4. When did you gain the assurance of salvation?

5. Was there a traumatic experience in your life that caused you to seek more of God?

6. Do you see any difference in the term seeking a Spirit-filled life and seeking more of God?

7. Have you experienced a time in your life when you felt like you were touched by the Holy Spirit? (e.g. the healing of the relationship between Ken and his father)

Assignment for next Week: What is my relationship with the Holy Spirit? Seek one example that you might share with the group next week.

Read: Chapter Two in *Confessions of a Non-Charismatic*
Faith:

    Prayer of Thanksgiving

    Song of commitment: *Spirit of the Living God*
Fellowship:

The true value of this study will be determined by the deepening of your relationship with God!

SESSION TWO: Dealing With Differences and Disappointments

Chapter 2   The Quiet One

Fellowship:

Ice breaker: Review names and share places of birth.

Faith:

Prayer of Adoration

Song of commitment: *Spirit of the Living God*

Facts:

Review: What did you observe the Holy Spirit doing in your life this past week?

Key Phrase: Warned by the Spirit

Introduction: We struggle with the desire to be different while longing to be identified as one of the group. Our human nature clearly dictates that regardless of our method of worship, we can rest assured that our method *is* the *right* method. The problem is that every other person is listening to *his* human nature with the same degree of certainty, and consequently, we have differences and battles ensue. In Chapter Two, *The Quiet One*, there are some classic examples of differences of opinions about how we should live and worship. License is contrasted with legalism, liturgy with free expression, and we forget that dwelling on contrasts or comparisons almost always has negative overtones and usually results in disappointments.

Disappointments in either ourselves or in others are painful. At those times when trouble seems overwhelming, it is critical to accept the comfort found in the words of Jesus in John 16:33. *"I have told you these things so that in me you may have peace. In this world you will have trouble. But take heart! I have overcome the world."*

Bible Reading: Ephesians 4:30-32 and John 7:24

Discovery and Discussion: One of the great challenges in Christian living is resolving differences. It is easy to act like a Christian, but it is much more difficult to *re-act* like one, especially when we are certain that we know what should be done. We react to the situation with our limited knowledge and proceed to operate on our incomplete information. How often we create misunderstanding in our lives and in the lives of those around us.

This is the time when we really need to use our seventh sense, the sense of God's will. The five senses are well recognized, developed, and satisfied to varying degrees. Continual attention is subconsciously given to the sixth sense as we strive to learn who we are and attempt to establish our own identity. But this seventh sense, the awareness of and interaction with God, is the greatest, but most allusive, sense of all.

Study Questions:

1. How do you react when someone does things totally different from the way you think they should be done?

2. How do you react when someone does not have the same convictions you have?

3. Do you have a Biblical basis for your reactions?

4. When you see someone is caught in sin, do you have stones in your hands?

5. What is the danger of judging? (Romans 2:1)

6. Criticism was a reality in the First Century church, as well as today's, and is not to be ignored. (Acts 6:1)

7. Who has the right to punish or make corrections? (John 8:7, Luke 6:42)

8. Who is in charge? (John 21:22)

9. Do you want a Spirit-filled life?

Assignment for next week: How can I develop my sensitivity to God's directions and open myself to become a channel through which the Holy Spirit can minister? How well do I recognize when the Holy Spirit is working in my life?

Read: Chapter Three in *Confessions of a Non-charismatic*

Faith:

Prayer of Thanksgiving

Song of commitment: *Spirit of the Living God*

Fellowship:

Anticipate becoming a new person. Start now!

SESSION THREE: Chosen for Ministry
Chapter 3 - God's Messenger to Northwest Iowa

Fellowship:

Icebreaker: Tell the place you met your best friend.

Faith:

Prayer of Adoration

Song of commitment: *Spirit of the Living God*

Facts:

Review: What ways did you discover for developing a greater awareness of the Holy Spirit at work in your life?

Key Phrase: Called by the Spirit

Introduction: Career changes are not unique to our generation. Beginning in the third chapter of Genesis and continuing on through the New Testament we read of individuals, families, and whole nations who relocated either by choice or necessity. Career changes usually followed. The Bible seldom reveals much about the family traumas associated with the many relocations mentioned. An excellent example which relates to Dr. J's move to Iowa is Genesis 12:1: *"The Lord said to Abram, Leave your country, your people and your father's household and go to the land I will show you . . . So Abram left."*

Bible Readings: Acts 13:2-4, Galatians 1:10

Discovery and Discussion: Have you ever considered under what conditions you would be willing to move? Have you considered moving away from family, friends, the neighborhood, and everything familiar to you? God calls and chooses, those to relocate who can meet a specific need or complete a task someplace else. Are they special people? I don't think so. If you have a plumbing problem, you call a plumber. Do you call him because he is a special person or because he has the skills needed to solve your problem? God does the same.

Study Questions:

1. Have you ever had a job relocation or modified your career?

2. Name some Bible characters who changed careers.

3. What does the issue of relocating have to do with the Spirit-filled life?

4. How do you resolve the differences if husband and wife do not agree about moving?

5. What is the role of church leaders in placing you in ministry?

6. How do you avoid trying to please people rather than God?

7. Will you be satisfied with less than God's best for you?

Assignment for next week: What are God's short-term plans for me, like now? Am I open to change?

Read: Chapter Four in *Confessions of a Non-charismatic*

Faith:

Prayer of Thanksgiving

Song of commitment: *Spirit of the Living God*

Fellowship:

The true value of this study will be determined by the deepening of your relationship with God!

SESSION FOUR: When the Pressure Is On
Chapter 4 - On the Spot

Fellowship:

Ice breaker: When did you become a Christian believer?

Faith:

Prayer of Adoration

Song of commitment: *Spirit of the Living God*

Facts:

Review: What did you learn about your short term-plans and/ or changes since the last sessiion?

Key Phrase: Strengthened by the Spirit

Introduction: It is difficult to keep our emotional balance when we are unexpectedly being asked questions that seem intended to put us on the defensive. It hurts even more when it comes from a fellow Christian believer. In a situation like the one presented in this chapter it can be difficult to react like a Christian. How blessed we are to have the Holy Spirit bringing to our minds exactly what is needed. The Holy Spirit may bring to your memory such verses as *"A gentle answer turns away wrath, but a harsh word stirs up anger."* Proverb 15:1, and James 1:19-20 *"Take note of this: Everyone should be quick to listen, slow to speak and slow to become angry for man's anger does not bring about the righteous life that God desires."*

Bible Readings: John 14:26, Romans 8:26-27, and Matthew 10:19-20

Discovery and Discussion: Seldom do we have much prayer time when we are placed on the spot. The Spirit knows our limitations and intercedes for us. He knows our heart, our intent, and our weakness. Examine your life right now and think of a time you were aware that someone was praying for you at that very moment. You may never know, but it could have been that the Spirit himself was praying for you.

Study Questions:

1. What physical reaction do you experience when you are on the spot?

2. How do you handle the pressure to defend yourself when you are challenged?

3. What can you do when you are a guest and you find it is not a friendly environment?

4. What steps do you need to take to be prepared to defend your faith?

5. What is spiritual warfare?

6. When should you excuse yourself from controversy?

7. It is a natural reaction to be pleased when you have accomplished a difficult assignment. How do you avoid gloating?

8. What changes are you willing to make to obtain a Spirit-filled life?

Assignment for next week: Remember the Beatitudes? Do I really live like I am blessed when the pressure is on?

Read: Chapter Five in *Confessions of a Non-charismatic*

Faith:

Prayer of Thanksgiving

Song of commitment: *Spirit of the Living God*

Fellowship:

Anticipate becoming a new person. Start now!

SESSION FIVE: Amazing Opportunities
Chapter 5 - Many Facets of Learning

Fellowship:

Icebreaker: Perhaps by this time the group will have bonded enough so that no further icebreakers will be needed.

Faith:

Prayer of Adoration

Song of commitment: *Spirit of the Living God*

Facts:

Review: What did you learn about your pressure tolerance?

Key Phrase: Compelled by the Spirit

Introduction: Learning is a lifelong experience. Traveling in more than 100 countries would be an education in itself, but Ken Anderson's life was truly enriched by the time spent with the Christian leaders he met on these travels. Ken found a singleness of purpose to glorify God as he strove to reach the nations for Christ. By sharing Christ's love, we see the denominational and theological differences fade as we proclaim the unity we share in Christ.

As Ken diligently sought the Spirit-filled life for which he longed, he learned much from colleagues living in different cultures with different Christian traditions. Language barriers were non-existent as they worshiped God in spirit and in truth. Yes, Ken was privileged to experience some amazing things and enjoyed the protection of the Holy Spirit as He opened and closed doors for Ken's ministry.

Bible Readings: 1 Corinthians 1:10, 10:31-11:1 and Acts 20:22

Discovery and Discussion: In our comfortable homes with so many of our wants satisfied, it is easy to close our eyes to the needs throughout the world. Our ears are closed so we can ignore the Macedonian cry, *"Come over and help us,"* even though our Macedonia may be only a few blocks or a few miles away. What will it take for us to feel compelled to go?

Our desire for completed plans with outlines and schedules all in place may interfere with a life of faith and trust in God. Our efforts are futile without His blessing. Our focus is blurred and distorted unless He charts the course. When He leads, He provides.

Study Questions:

1. What is your attitude when different Biblical interpretations are presented?

2. Do you tolerate or appreciate Christians with opinions that are different from your own?

3. How did you acquire your style of worship? Is it Biblically based?

4. How do you determine which door of opportunity has been opened by the Holy Spirit?

5. How do you avoid coming under bondage to others?

6. What can we do collectively to avoid becoming calloused to the suffering in Third World countries?

7. What can I or we do to alleviate the suffering of one family in our own neighborhood?

8. Are you ready to walk by faith and trust God to guide you into the Spirit-filled life?

Assignment for next week: What do I feel compelled to do for Christ? What changes must I make to be a better example for others to see Christ?

Read: Chapter Six in *Confessions of a Non-charismatic*

Faith:

Prayer of Thanksgiving

Song of commitment: *Spirit of the Living God*

Fellowship:

The true value of this study will be determined by the deepening of your relationship with God

SESSION SIX: Honesty Is Humility

Chapter 6 - Martyrs and My Pride Syndrome

Fellowship:

Faith:

>Prayer of Adoration
>
>Song of commitment: *Spirit of the Living God*

Facts:

>**Review:** What do you think about learning through serving?
>
>**Key Phrase:** Convicted by the Spirit
>
>**Introduction:** Pride is one of the most insidious deterrents to
a Spirit-filled life. Self-respect seems so justifiable, but it is so easy to
slip across the line into self-exaltation. Pride displayed in any manner
damages our Christian witness. But it is equally unwise to engage in
self-abasement for false humility is equally unwelcome. A false
evaluation, either too high or too low, is dishonest. Honesty is humility
and humility is honesty.
>
>On Ken's trip to Uganda his heart was deeply moved by his
visit to the death chambers created by the former proud arrogant dictator.
We can only wonder just how many thousands of Christians were
martyred there. Who can fathom the depths to which we can plunge
without the restraining power of God? In Jeremiah 17:9 we have this
frightening declaration, *"The heart is deceitful above all things and
beyond cure.Who can understand it?"* Through this experience, Ken
was convicted of his own sinful pride and asked God for forgiveness.
>
>Humility has a great reward. It is a secret key to a Spirit-filled
life! *"If my people, who are called by my name, will* humble
*themselves and pray and seek my face and turn from their wicked
ways, then will I hear from heaven and will forgive their sin and
will heal their land."* 2 Chronicles 7:14.
>
>**Bible Readings:** Philippians 1:29 and Proverbs 18:12
>
>**Discovery and Discussion:** It is difficult to think of pride

and sacrifice at the same time for they are at such opposite extremes. But the Bible reveals both, one with consequences, the other with commendation. Consequence: *"Pride goes before destruction, a haughty spirit before a fall."* Proverbs 16:18. Commendation: *"Greater love has no one than this, that he lay down his life for his friends."* John 15:13. Every Christian martyr has demonstrated that level of love. There is no better friend than Jesus Christ!

In Acts 7:60 we have the story of Stephen, the first Christian martyr. He pronounced the depth of his commitment when he prayed, *"Lord, do not hold this sin against them."* Only God could enable an individual to love like that. Paul wrote of suffering for Christ's sake as a privilege. *"For it was granted to you on behalf of Christ not only to believe on him, but also to suffer for him."* Philippians 1:29.

Study Questions:

1. Is pride a problem at all levels of society?

2. What is your greatest area of pride - possessions, intellect, personality, looks, power, achievements?

3. What do you think you are willing to die for?

4. How can the sin of pride be avoided?

5. How do you express humility without appearing proud?

6. Am I holding onto anything that would keep me from enjoying a Spirit-filled life?

Assignment for next week: What would I discover if I sought humility and righteousness? How do I deny my self-centeredness?

Read: Chapter Seven in *Confessions of a Non-charismatic*

Faith:

Prayer of Thanksgiving

Song of commitment: *Spirit of the Living God*

Fellowship:

Anticipate becoming a new person. Start now!

SESSION SEVEN: Total Commitment
Chapter 7 - Facing Martyrdom

Fellowship:

Faith:

> Prayer of Adoration
>
> Song of commitment: *Spirit of the Living God*

Facts:

> **Review:** What are your thoughts about humility and honesty?
>
> **Key Phrase:** Helped by the Spirit
>
> **Introduction:** It is one thing to talk about martyrs, but it's extremely difficult to imagine what it must feel like to face martyrdom. Can you comprehend what love you must have to stay behind and face martyrdom when you could escape? In Ken's conversation with Jonathan Lee in his home in Tientsin, his heart was quickened. Mr. Lee knew trouble and even death was inevitable; to see him wait for it to come to his household challenged Ken's commitment to Christ.
>
> Remember Stephen? Whether or not he understood the depth of the animosity of his listeners, he continued with his testimony. What power he possessed and what power possessed him! Stephen was full of the Holy Spirit. Those who saw him said his face was like that of an angel. Acts 8:1: "*And Saul was there, giving approval to his death.*"
>
> **Bible Readings:** Hebrews 13:6, Philippians 1:21
>
> **Discovery and Discussion:** Without knowing the rest of the story about Stephen, it leaves us feeling empty, but there is more. Likewise, we will never know the impact of Mr. and Mrs. Jonathan Lee until we join them in the celestial city. But we do know what followed after Stephen was martyred. The change was not immediate. In fact, Saul kept spewing out his murderous threats for some time, and he went on to secure power to arrest those of "The Way". But God!
>
> The entire history of the Christian church was changed that day on the Damascus Road when Saul was surrounded by a light

from heaven. Or did the change begin when Saul saw Stephen's faithfulness even through martyrdom?

It is impossible for us to measure the impact of the life of Paul. It is equally impossible for us to measure the impact that the life and death of Stephen had on Paul. Stephen's life is an extreme example of personal evangelism, but the power of his sacrifice continues on. Paul wrote in 2 Corinthians 3:3, *"You show that you are a letter from Christ, the result of our ministry, written not with ink, but with the Spirit of God, not on tablets of stone but on tablets of human hearts."*

Study Questions:

1. What help do you need to be more involved/prepared for personal evangelism?
2. What responsibility do we have to learn about Christian persecution?
3. What should we do about religious freedom around the world?
4. What is the relationship of prayer to a Spirit-filled life?
5. What can we do to increase our effectiveness in prayer?
6. Can you fathom what your life could be like when you are living a Spirit-filled life?

Assignment for next week: How can I develop awareness that people around me need Jesus? What am I willing to sacrifice to demonstrate my total commitment to God?

Read: Chapter Eight in *Confessions of a Non-charismatic*

Faith:

Prayer of Thanksgiving

Song of commitment: *Spirit of the Living God*

Fellowship:

The true value of this study will be determined by the deepening of your relationship with God!

SESSION EIGHT: Fruit of the Spirit
Chapter 8 - The Holy Spirit at Work

Fellowship:

Faith:

Prayer of Adoration

Song of commitment: *Spirit of the Living God*

Facts:

Review: What did you discover as you contemplated a Spirit-filled life?

Key Phrase: Blessed by the Spirit

Introduction: If you have observed that it is easier to grow weeds than to grow grass, you won't be surprised that fruit of the Spirit is singular but lusts of the flesh is plural. When Jesus healed the ten lepers, only one came back to say thanks. Do you begin to get the feeling that it is easier to be negative than positive? Sad but true!

Consider an average day for you or any of your acquaintances. How many times do you complain compared with the number of your expressions of gratitude? Most of us do not follow the instruction, *"In everything give thanks."* (1 Thessalonians 5:18). Perhaps our negative comments happen because we have been taught to look for problems and find solutions.

Ken shared his experience with the Chinese pastor as they were *"praising the Lord"* together. It was a freeing of his spirit. You may want to try it. A friend who is active in gospel music liked to encourage a congregation in worship with Bible verses such as: *"O God,* may *all the peoples praise you"* (Psalm 67:3) or *"Praise the Lord, O my soul"* (Psalm 146:1) Then as he introduced the song *Praise Him, Praise Him,* he suggested they should try to feel grumpy as they sang the first verse. They couldn't do it. Something happens as you praise the Lord. The Holy Spirit is at work within us!

Bible Readings: Psalm 150:6, Galatians 5:22-23, John

chapters 14-16

Discovery and Discussion: Another exciting evidence of the Holy Spirit at work in your life is the growth of the fruit of the Spirit. They are not add-ons. They come from within.

Examine your life carefully for one week to see if you are *living* in the fruit of the Spirit. Make a chart listing each of the fruit listed in Galatians 5:22. Every day on a scale of one to ten, rank yourself on each of the nine categories. As the week progresses, check your attitude and behavior. The quality will not change for each fruit is from the Holy Spirit, but the quantity revealed may change drastically.

Growth of the fruit of the Spirit in your life is certainly a reason for praise.

Study Questions:

1. Have you ever participated in a mass rally for Christ?
2. Have you been in church services when a public invitation to accept Christ was given? Did anyone respond? What was your reaction?
3. Have you been in services when your heart was *"strangely warmed"* and you felt close to God?
4. How or when do you find it easiest to praise God?
5. What proof do you have of the fruit of the Spirit in your life?
6. Which fruit are most prominent in your life? Least apparent?
7. How do you see praise related to a Spirit-filled life?

Assignment for next week: How can I become aware of the fruit of the Spirit growing in my life?

Read: Chapter Nine in *Confessions of a Non-charismatic*

Faith:

Prayer of Thanksgiving

Song of commitment: *Spirit of the Living God*

Fellowship:

Anticipate becoming a new person. Start now!

SESSION NINE: Finding Answers
Chapter 9 - Discovering Heavenly Places

Fellowship:

Faith:

Prayer of Adoration

Song of commitment: *Spirit of the Living God*

Facts:

Review: Were there changes in your attitude or behavior as a result of considering the fruit of the Spirit?

Key Phrase: Directed by the Spirit

Introduction: Sometimes the answer to a question is too obvious to be recognized. For years Ken had been seeking the Spirit-filled life. He had read the complete book of Joshua many times, but on that day high above the Pacific Ocean, it was as if he was reading it for the first time. Those three words, OBSERVE TO DO, were like a guide beckoning him to follow. It was more than that. It was a command. He felt directed to meditate on His Word, God's Word, and do exactly what it said! Ken knew then he had the key to living a genuinely Spirit-filled life.

A key can only unlock the door. The responsibility for opening and entering through the door was his. The Bible was not something he had avoided, but those words suddenly came with a new sense of urgency. It was more than study. It included action. There is work to be done if we are to enjoy the Spirit-filled life.

Bible Readings: Philippians 4:8, Proverbs 1:1-7, Isaiah 40:31

Discovery and Discussion: An old Chinese proverb states the power of a thought. "Sow a thought, reap an act. Sow an act, reap a habit. Sow a habit, reap a character. Sow a character, reap a destiny." If you can control your thoughts, you are in control of your life.

"As he thinks within his heart, so is he." (Proverbs 23:7) is the Bible's way of saying actions speak louder than words. Words may

cover for the moment, but over time we live out our true self. *"Out of the overflow of the heart the mouth speaks."* (Matthew 12:34)

It is one thing to discover heavenly places, but it is a greater blessing to dwell there. The secret is found in Isaiah 26:3: *"You will keep him in perfect peace whose mind is stayed on You: because he trusts in You."*

Study Questions:

1. How much time do you spend reading and studying the Bible?
2. Do you have a plan for Bible study?
3. What do you find most difficult about staying in the Bible?
4. Is it difficult to maintain a Spirit-filled life without Bible study?
5. When you read or study your Bible, do you feel closer to God?
6. Do you need help in interpreting the Bible?
7. What is the difference between meditating on the Bible and Bible study?
8. How do you know you are living a Spirit-filled life?

Questions for the week: How do I control my thoughts? How can I learn to efficiently memorize Scripture?

Read: Chapter Ten in *Confessions of a Non-charismatic*

Faith:

Prayer of Thanksgiving

Song of commitment: *Spirit of the Living God*

Fellowship:

The true value of this study will be determined by the deepening of your relationship with God!

SESSION TEN: Spiritual Renewal
Chapter 10 - Charismatic Renaissance

Fellowship:

Faith:

Prayer of Adoration

Song of commitment: *Spirit of the Living God*

Facts:

Review: Did your attitude change as you spent time thinking on the fruit of the Spirit?

Key Phrase: Challenged by the Spirit

Introduction: It is difficult to understand why for centuries there was little emphasis placed on the Holy Spirit or His manifestations. It seems that with the rise of the clergy as a Christian separate from the laity, and as the church became more institutionalized, there was less opportunity for these spiritual gifts to be exercised in public worship. Consequently, they lost significance in the lives of church members.

The renaissance of the charismatic manifestation at the turn of the twentieth century was a phenomenon that began outside of the control of the organized churches. Because it did not originate among the clergy, it was suspect and languished with criticism and derision as Ken shared in chapter two. Nevertheless, several denominations were born in those early prayer meetings and have flourished, now having members numbering in the millions world-wide.

Another thrust of the Holy Spirit through special manifestations came again in the mid-sixties. It was called the Charismatic Renewal and made a special impact in the Episcopal and Roman Catholic Churches. Since then the interest in the Holy Spirit and the Spirit-filled life has intensified.

Bible Readings: John 14:16 and 1 Corinthians 3:1-3

Discovery and Discussion: For more than a half-century Ken sought God's fullness. He longed to know Him better. The division created by emphasis on special gifts disturbed him greatly, and he prayed that we might all be one in the Spirit. The motive for this book has been to share his heart-cry for all that God has for us, regardless of denominational differences. Through his search for the Spirit-filled life, Ken has learned that the Holy Spirit continues to distribute His gifts according to His good pleasure. He also learned that fellowship between those called *charismatics* and those who do not bear that name can be rich and blessed for we are serving the same Triune God. Read 1 Corinthians 12 and 13 carefully, prayerfully, and without a desire to prove any personal bias. Notice the first sentence in 13:1: *"And now I will show you the most excellent way."* Chapter 13 has been termed the Love Chapter. It speaks for itself.

Study Questions:

1. How does *charismatic* relate to the church?
2. What manifestations are commonly associated with the *charismatic movement*?
3. What are the *doctrines* of the church?
4. Does *milk* refer to the doctrines of the church?
5. What does it mean to be worldly?
6. How do I attain spiritual maturity?
7. What changes must occur for me to truly enjoy a Spirit-filled life?

Assignment for next week: What are my responsibilities for ministry in the body of Christ?

Read: Chapter 11 in *Confessions of a Non-charismatic*

Faith:
Prayer of Thanksgiving
Song of commitment: *Spirit of the Living God*

Fellowship:

Anticipate becoming a new person. Start now!

SESSION ELEVEN: Prepared for a Purpose
Chapter 11 - The Spirit-filled Life

Fellowship:

Faith:

> Prayer of Adoration
>
> Song of commitment: *Spirit of the Living God*

Facts:

> **Review:** Share what you believe to be your gifts.
>
> **Key Phrase:** Commissioned by Christ, Empowered by the

Spirit

Introduction: If you were asked, "Do you feel ordinary or special?" a likely response would be "Compared with what?" I ask the question because we seem to think God has special jobs for special people. Does that mean he has ordinary jobs for ordinary people? Who is ordinary in His eyes?

Every person is special in God's eyes, and to us His followers, His disciples, He entrusted a challenging task for us to accomplish. We were commissioned by Christ with these words from Matthew 28:19-20: *"Go and make disciples of all nations, baptizing them in the name of the Father and of the Son and of the Holy Spirit, and teaching them to obey everything I have commanded you. And surely I am with you always, to the very end of the age."*

That is the assignment, and He has plans that will enable us to complete the mission. Christ knew our limitations and promised help would arrive after He went away. He assured us that if we would wait we could have the gift the Father had promised, the gift of the Holy Spirit, a Spirit-filled life. Our faith in Christ prepares us for service, but it is the gift of the Holy Spirit that empowers us to get the job done. *"You will receive power when the Holy Spirit comes on you; and you will be my witnesses in Jerusalem, and in all Judea and Samaria, and to the ends of the earth."* (Acts 1:8)

The commission was given to the disciples collectively. *"Now you are the body of Christ, and each one of you is a part of it."* (I Corinthians 12: 27) In this body He has placed each of us where He wants us to be. Reaching the ends of the earth with the gospel is a cooperative effort and we are to function like a body with each one using the gift they received. Paul planted, Apollo watered, but God gave the increase. There is no place for spectators in this work force.

Bible Readings: Jeremiah 29:11-13, 1 Corinthians 12:27-31

Discovery and Discussion: We have the commission and have been gifted for service. We know where the power can be obtained to get the task done. We have observed and learned what and how. Now we are to be obedient *to do,* using the resources He has provided.

Study Questions:

1. Were some gifts only for the early church?
2. Is it wrong to ask for specific gifts? (1 Corinthians 12:31)
3. What is the difference between natural ability and a spiritual gift?
4. How do I cope with the gifts I have if my church doesn't use them?
5. Does every Christian have a spiritual gift? (1 Corinthians 12:7, 13)
6. What is the relationship between spiritual gifts and a Spirit-filled life?
7. Should every congregation have all the gifts among its members?
8. Am I willing to accept God's gift of the Holy Spirit?

Assignment for next week: What are my responsibilities to minister in the body of Christ? What gifts could I be using more effectively? How? What is my purpose in God's kingdom?

Read: Chapter 12 in *Confessions of a Non-charismatic*
Faith:

Prayer of Thanksgiving
Song of commitment: *Spirit of the Living God*

Fellowship:

The true value of this study will be determined
by the deepening of your relationship with God!

SESSION TWELVE: Maintaining a Spirit-filled Life
Chapter 12 - The Stockholm Experience

Fellowship:
Faith:

Prayer of Adoration

Song of commitment: *Spirit of the Living God*

Facts:

Review: What steps have you been taking to seek a Spirit-filled life?

Key Phrase: Sustained by the Spirit

Introduction: This is our last session and time for celebration. The report of Ken's journey begun in chapter one is completed in this, the last chapter. His desired goal was reached, but the journey is not over. He found what he was seeking: A Spirit-filled life. Ahead is the next stage of the Christian journey. It is the wonderful experience of walking with God endued with the power of the Holy Spirit. The final stop will be the face-to-face meeting with Christ in the celestial city.

This book has been an open and honest sharing of a search for the Spirit-filled life. It is now important to review or summarize Ken's steps in reaching the climax of his search.

Revealing his misery as well as his ministry has made this a believable experience. Anyone who is seeking a Spirit-filled life can identify with his struggles. It provides insights on achieving the victories. He never lost sight of the goal: To have all that God has for him.

Throughout the book no formula is presented for attaining the goal, yet it seems there are some steps which are quite clear. The first marked change came after his confession of his hatred for his father. This demonstrated the impact of correcting troubled relationships. Equally penitent was his cry to God *"work me over . . . including my motives, attitudes, and sensitivities."*

Reading the words, *Observe to do,* appears to have been his major turning point. Ken described the impact of those three words in this manner: *"In those three words, I found the key to living a genuinely Spirit-filled life . . . ."*

Regarding the alignment of his desires with God's desires, he wrote, *"Once more the Holy Spirit, the Comforter who Jesus had promised was calling me . . . yes, guiding me . . . into the way to obtain and maintain a spirit-filled life,"*

This last chapter contains two extremes: the greatest rebuke and the greatest blessing. There may be a close relationship between the two. The sudden realization that even his devotion to God was tainted by his own selfish desire for personal comfort may have produced a deeper sense of humility.

One can never be certain why reflections produce the responses that come. Ken Anderson offers no explanation for the emotional impact that occurred as he was reflecting on what God had allowed him to experience on that world tour. But he was overwhelmed with an extended expression of praise. Afterwards he expressed an unusual sense of feeling clean. He wrote, *"After my total submission to God, I was experiencing the fullness of God's presence. I was beginning to know the joy of the Spirit-filled life."*

Bible Readings: John 16:13, Philippians 1:6, Hebrews 12:1, Revelation 2:10, 26

Discovery and Discussion: The moment of complete surrender is a new beginning. Those things which enable us to reach a

147

life committed to God must continue if this relationship is to be sustained. The keys to the Spirit-filled life are true humility, Biblical obedience, aligned desires, and total submission to God. This study's true value will be determined by how closely we each walk with God through the power of the Holy Spirit.

Study Questions:

1. Do you have a better understanding of the process of seeking a Spirit-filled life?

2. What difference has this study made in your life?

Faith:

      Prayer of Thanksgiving

      Song of commitment: *Spirit of the Living God*

Fellowship:

Anticipate becoming a new person. Start now!

Spirit of the Living God

LIVING GOD   Irregular

Daniel Iverson, 1935; adapted   Daniel Iverson, 1935

Spir - it of the liv - ing God, Fall a-fresh on me;

Spir - it of the liv - ing God, Fall a-fresh on me.

Melt me, mold me, Fill me, use me.

Spir - it of the liv - ing God, Fall a-fresh on me.

149